KRISHNA MOHAN
AVANCHA

Brand Mastery: How to
Build a Beloved Brand That
Captivates Hearts and
Drives Success

Contents

Chapter 1: Introduction: The Power of Building a Brand

What we will be covering in this chapter:

- Understanding the significance of building a brand
- Exploring the benefits of a strong brand identity

Understanding the significance of building a brand:

In today's competitive business landscape, building a brand has become more important than ever before. A brand is not just a logo, a name, or a slogan; it is the perception and reputation that consumers have of a company or product. Building a strong brand involves crafting a unique identity, establishing a compelling brand image, and fostering positive associations in the minds of consumers. Here are some key reasons why building a brand is significant:

Differentiation: A well-built brand helps a company stand out from its competitors. In crowded markets, where multiple businesses offer similar products or services, a strong brand sets a company apart by highlighting its unique selling points and value proposition. It creates a distinct and memorable identity that helps consumers recognize and remember the brand.

Trust and credibility: Building a reputable brand fosters trust and credibility among consumers. When people have confidence in a brand, they are more likely to choose its products or services over those of competitors. A strong brand conveys reliability, quality, and consistency, establishing a positive perception that encourages customer loyalty and repeat business.

Emotional connection: Brands that successfully connect with their target audience on an emotional level have a significant advantage. By appealing to consumers' emotions, a brand can create a deep and lasting relationship with its customers. Emotional branding goes beyond functional benefits and taps into the values, aspirations, and desires of consumers, forging a strong bond that extends beyond mere transactions.

Price premium: A well-established brand allows a company to command a price premium for its products or services. When consumers perceive a brand as prestigious, reliable, or superior, they are often willing to pay more for it. By building a brand that is associated with quality and value, businesses can increase their profit margins and achieve higher profitability.

Customer loyalty and advocacy: A strong brand cultivates customer loyalty, resulting in repeat purchases and positive word-of-mouth recommendations. When consumers have a positive experience with a brand and feel a sense of affinity towards it, they become brand advocates, willingly promoting the brand to their friends, family, and social networks. This organic form of marketing can significantly enhance a company's reach and reputation.

Competitive advantage: Building a brand provides a sustainable competitive advantage. While competitors can replicate products or services, it is much harder to replicate a brand's reputation, customer loyalty, and emotional connection. A strong brand acts as a moat, protecting a company from competitors and creating barriers to entry.

Exploring the benefits of a strong brand identity:

A strong brand identity goes beyond a recognizable logo or visual elements. It encompasses the core values, personality, and purpose of a brand. Here are some benefits of establishing a strong brand identity:

Recognition and recall: A well-defined brand identity makes a brand easily recognizable and memorable. Consistent use of visual elements, such as logos, colors, typography, and imagery, creates familiarity among consumers. This recognition and recall help the brand cut through the clutter of competitors and stand out in consumers' minds.

Consistency and coherence: A strong brand identity ensures consistency across all touchpoints and communication channels. From advertising campaigns to packaging and customer service, a consistent brand identity helps create a coherent brand experience. This consistency builds trust and reinforces the brand's values and promises.

Brand loyalty and advocacy: A strong brand identity fosters brand loyalty. When consumers resonate with a brand's identity and values, they are more likely to develop a long-term relationship with the brand. Loyal customers become advocates, spreading positive word-of-mouth and defending the brand during challenging times.

Attracting the right audience: A well-defined brand identity helps attract the right target audience. By clearly communicating the brand's values, personality, and positioning, it becomes easier for consumers who align with those attributes to identify and connect with the brand. This leads to a more engaged and loyal customer base.

Flexibility and adaptability: A strong brand identity provides a framework for flexibility and adaptability. While the core elements of the brand identity remain consistent, the brand can evolve and adapt to changing market trends and consumer preferences. This flexibility allows the brand to stay relevant and maintain its competitive edge.

Brand extensions and diversification: A strong brand identity opens up opportunities for brand extensions and diversification. When a brand has built a strong reputation and established trust, it can leverage its identity to expand into new product lines or enter new markets. Consumers are more likely to accept and embrace brand extensions because of their existing positive associations with the brand.

In conclusion, building a brand and establishing a strong brand identity are crucial for businesses aiming to succeed in today's competitive market-place. A strong brand sets a company apart from its competitors, builds trust and credibility, creates emotional connections with consumers, and fosters customer loyalty and advocacy. Moreover, a strong brand identity ensures recognition, consistency, and coherence, attracting the right audience and providing opportunities for growth and diversi-fication. Investing in building a brand is a long-term strategy that can yield significant benefits and contribute to the overall success and sustainability of a business.

Chapter 2: Defining Your Brand Vision and Values

W hat we will be covering in this chapter:

- Clarifying your brand's purpose and mission
- Identifying the core values that will guide your brand

2 / 2

Clarifying your brand's purpose and mission is essential for establishing a strong foundation and direction for your business. It serves as a compass, guiding all your actions and decisions, and helps you differentiate yourself from competitors. Additionally, identifying the core values that will guide your brand is crucial in building a meaningful and authentic connection with your target audience. In this elaborative content, we will explore the importance of clarifying your brand's purpose and mission, as well as the process of identifying core values to shape your brand identity.

Clarifying Your Brand's Purpose and Mission

Your brand's purpose is the reason why your business exists beyond making a profit. It reflects the impact you aim to have on the world and the specific problem you aim to solve. Defining your purpose requires introspection and a deep understanding of your business, industry, and target audience. Here are some key steps to clarify your brand's purpose and mission:

Evaluate your business: Start by analyzing your products or services and identifying the value they provide. Consider how your offerings address a specific need or solve a problem for your customers.

Understand your target audience: Gain insights into your target audience's desires, pain points, and aspirations. Determine how your brand can contribute to their lives or make a positive difference.

Define your brand's impact: Reflect on the broader

impact you wish to achieve beyond serving customers. Consider the social, environmental, or cultural contributions your brand can make to society.

Craft a purpose statement: Once you have a clear understanding of your business, target audience, and impact, distill your purpose into a concise and inspiring statement. This purpose statement should communicate the essence of why your brand exists and the change you want to bring about.

Align internal stakeholders: Ensure that your purpose resonates with your team members and stakeholders. Involve them in the process and gather their input to foster a shared sense of purpose and commitment.

Remember that your brand's purpose should be authentic, credible, and aligned with your business capabilities. It should resonate with your customers and inspire them to connect with your brand on a deeper level.

Identifying the Core Values that Will Guide Your Brand

Core values serve as guiding principles that shape

your brand's behavior, culture, and decision-making processes. These values represent what your brand stands for and act as a moral compass for your organization. Here's a step-by-step approach to identifying core values for your brand:

Reflect on your brand's personality: Consider the traits and characteristics that define your brand's identity. Think about how you want your brand to be perceived by others and what values are important in achieving that perception.

Evaluate your current values: Assess the existing values and beliefs that drive your business. Determine which ones align with your desired brand image and discard or refine those that don't.

Involve your team: Conduct workshops or brainstorming sessions with your team to identify the values they believe are important for the brand. Encourage open discussions and collaboration to gain diverse perspectives.

Consider your target audience: Reflect on the values that resonate with your target audience. Research their preferences and align your brand values with their aspirations and expectations.

Select a set of core values: From the ideas generated through the previous steps, distill a set of core values that represent the essence of your brand. Aim for a concise list of values that are memorable, meaningful, and actionable.

Integrate values into your brand: Once you have identified your core values, integrate them into every aspect of your brand. From internal processes to external communications, ensure that your values are consistently expressed and demonstrated.

Remember that core values should be more than just buzzwords; they should be embedded in your brand's culture and reflected in your actions. Living up to your core values helps build trust, credibility, and long-term loyalty with your customers.

In conclusion, clarifying your brand's purpose and mission is crucial for providing a clear direction and establishing a meaningful connection with your audience. Identifying core values that align with your brand's purpose ensures consistent decision-making and behavior, fostering trust and loyalty. By clearly defining your brand's purpose and living up to your core values, you can differentiate yourself in the marketplace and build a strong and authentic brand identity.

Framework for Creating a Brand's Purpose and Mission Statement:

Research and Analysis:

Understand the target audience: Conduct market research and identify the needs, aspirations, and pain points of your target audience.

Evaluate the competitive landscape: Analyze competitors to identify gaps and opportunities in the market.

Assess your own strengths and capabilities: Identify what sets your brand apart and how it can add unique value.

Define Your Brand's DNA:

Identify your brand's personality: Determine the traits, values, and emotions you want your brand to embody.

Craft a brand positioning statement: Clearly define how your brand is different and better than competitors in a concise statement.

Identify the Brand's Purpose:

Explore the bigger picture: Reflect on the positive impact your brand can have on customers, society, or the world.

Define the problem you aim to solve: Identify a specific challenge or need that your brand is uniquely positioned to address.

Formulate a purpose statement: Craft a compelling and concise statement that captures the reason for your brand's existence and the change it seeks to bring about.

Example:

Let's consider a hypothetical scenario where a new brand is born in the fitness industry.

Research and Analysis:

The target audience is health-conscious individuals who prioritize physical fitness and seek convenient workout solutions.

The fitness industry is crowded, but there is a lack of accessible and personalized fitness options for busy professionals.

The brand's strengths lie in its team of expert trainers, innovative technology, and commitment to customer convenience.

Define Your Brand's DNA:

The brand aims to embody traits such as expertise, personalization, convenience, and motivation.

Brand Positioning Statement: "We are a tech-powered fitness brand that brings personalized workouts and expert guidance to your doorstep, empowering busy professionals to achieve their fitness goals conveniently and effectively."

Identify the Brand's Purpose:

Bigger picture: The brand believes that everyone deserves access to personalized fitness solutions, regardless of their hectic schedules.

Problem to solve: Address the challenge of limited time and accessibility by delivering tailored workouts and expert guidance at the customer's convenience.

Purpose Statement: "Our purpose is to revolutionize fitness by making personalized workouts and expert guidance accessible to busy professionals, empowering them to prioritize their health and achieve their fitness goals on their terms."

In this example, the brand's purpose and mission statement clearly communicate its commitment to making fitness accessible, convenient, and personalized for busy professionals. This purpose serves as a guiding principle for the brand's actions, strategies, and customer interactions.

To bring the brand to life, it would be essential to align all brand elements, such as the logo, visual identity, messaging, and customer experience, with the purpose and mission statement. This can be achieved through consistent communication, targeted marketing campaigns, and delivering exceptional customer experiences that reflect the brand's values and purpose. Over time, the brand's reputation, customer base, and market position would grow, solidifying its presence in the fitness industry.

3

Chapter 3: Conducting Market Research

W hat we will be covering in this chapter:

- Understanding your target audience and their needs
- Analyzing market trends and competition

Understanding Your Target Audience and Their Needs

To effectively reach and engage your target audience, it is crucial to have a deep understanding of who they are and what they need. By understanding your target audience, you can tailor your products, services, and marketing efforts to meet their specific requirements, ultimately increasing your chances of success. Here are some key steps to help you gain a comprehensive understanding of your target audience and their needs:

Conduct Market Research: Start by conducting thorough market research to gather data and insights about your target audience. This research can involve surveys, focus groups, interviews, and analyzing existing customer data. The goal is to gather information about their demographics, interests, behaviors, and purchasing patterns.

Create Buyer Personas: Once you have collected sufficient data, develop buyer personas that represent different segments of your target audience. A buyer persona is a semi-fictional representation of your ideal customer, including details about their age, gender, occupation, motivations, challenges, and goals. These personas help you understand your audience on a more personal level.

Identify Pain Points and Motivations: Dig deeper into your target audience's pain points, challenges, and motivations. What problems are they trying to solve? What goals are they trying to achieve? By identifying these factors, you can position your products or services as solutions that directly address their needs and desires.

Monitor Online Conversations: Social media platforms, forums, and online communities are great sources for monitoring discussions related to your industry, products, or services. By actively listening to these conversations, you can gain valuable insights into what your target audience is talking about, their opinions, and their pain points.

Analyze Customer Feedback: Pay close attention to feedback from your existing customers. Customer reviews, testimonials, and feedback forms can provide valuable information about their experiences, satisfaction levels, and areas for improvement. This feedback can help you refine your offerings to better meet their needs.

Analyzing Market Trends and Competition

Understanding market trends and competition is essential for staying ahead in any industry. By analyzing market trends, you can identify opportunities and adapt your strategies to meet changing consumer demands. Similarly, studying your competition allows you to gain insights into their strengths and weaknesses, helping you differentiate yourself and position your brand more effectively. Here are some steps to effectively analyze market trends and competition:

Track Industry News: Stay updated with the latest news, developments, and innovations in your industry. Subscribe to industry publications, blogs, and newsletters to receive regular updates. By staying informed, you can identify emerging trends, new technologies, and changing consumer preferences.

Monitor Consumer Behavior: Keep a close eye on consumer behavior patterns and shifts. Changes in consumer preferences, buying habits, and expectations can provide valuable insights into market trends. Utilize tools like surveys, focus groups, and market research reports to understand the evolving needs and desires of your target audience.

Conduct Competitor Analysis: Study your competitors to identify their strategies, strengths, weaknesses, and unique selling propositions. Analyze their products or services, pricing strategies, marketing campaigns, customer experience, and online presence. This analysis can help you identify areas where you can differentiate yourself and capitalize on untapped market opportunities.

Use Data Analytics: Leverage data analytics tools to gather and analyze relevant data. This includes analyzing website traffic, social media engagement, conversion rates, and customer feedback. Data-driven insights can provide a comprehensive view of market trends and help you make informed decisions.

Attend Industry Events and Conferences: Participate in industry events, conferences, and trade shows to network with peers, industry leaders, and potential customers. These events provide opportunities to learn about the latest trends, connect with like-minded professionals, and gain insights from keynote speakers.

By understanding your target audience and their needs, as well as analyzing market trends and competition, you can develop strategies that resonate with your customers and give you a competitive edge. Continuous monitoring and adaptation are key to staying relevant and successful in today's dynamic business landscape.

4

Chapter 4: Creating a Memorable Brand Name and Logo

W hat we will be covering in this chapter:

- Developing a brand name that resonates with your target audience
- Designing a visually appealing and recognizable logo

Developing a Brand Name that Resonates with Your Target Audience

When it comes to developing a brand name, it's crucial to create something that not only represents your business but also resonates with your target audience. A well-crafted brand name can capture attention, create an emotional connection, and leave a lasting impression on your customers. Here are some key considerations to keep in mind when developing a brand name that resonates with your target audience:

Understand Your Target Audience: Before you start brainstorming brand name ideas, it's essential to have a deep understanding of your target audience. Research their demographics, interests, values, and preferences. This knowledge will help you create a brand name that speaks directly to them.

Reflect Your Brand Identity: Your brand name should reflect your brand's values, personality, and unique selling proposition. Consider the core message you want to convey and choose a name that aligns with it. Whether it's being professional, innovative, or playful, your brand name should set the right tone.

Keep it Simple and Memorable: A brand name that is simple and easy to remember is more likely to resonate with your audience. Avoid complex or lengthy names that can be confusing or easily forgotten. Aim for brevity and clarity to make your brand name instantly recognizable.

Be Authentic and Unique: In a crowded market-place, it's essential to stand out from the competition. Develop a brand name that is authentic to your business and differentiates you from others. Avoid generic or cliché names that blend in with the crowd. Conduct thorough research to ensure your chosen name is not already in use or trademarked.

Consider Cultural and Linguistic Nuances: If you plan to expand your brand globally or target specific cultural groups, consider cultural and linguistic nuances. Ensure that your brand name does not have negative connotations or unintended meanings in different languages or cultural contexts. Conduct thorough research or consult with experts to avoid any potential pitfalls.

Designing a Visually Appealing and Recognizable Logo

Once you have a compelling brand name, the next step is to design a visually appealing and recognizable logo. A logo serves as the visual representation of your brand, and it plays a crucial role in creating brand recognition and communicating your brand's identity. Here are some important factors to consider when designing your logo:

Simplicity is Key: A simple and clean logo design tends to be more memorable and versatile. Avoid complex designs that may be difficult to reproduce or understand. Keep in mind that your logo should be easily recognizable even when scaled down or displayed in black and white.

Reflect Your Brand Identity: Your logo should visually communicate your brand's identity, values, and personality. Consider the emotions and associations you want your brand to evoke. Whether it's trust, creativity, or excitement, choose colors, fonts, and shapes that align with your brand's essence.

Make it Timeless: While it's important to stay current and relevant, it's also crucial to design a logo that stands the test of time. Avoid trendy design elements that may quickly become outdated. Aim for a timeless look that can represent your brand for years to come.

Versatility and Scalability: Your logo will be used across various mediums, from digital platforms to print materials. Ensure that your logo is versatile and scalable, meaning it looks good and maintains its clarity and impact whether it's displayed on a large billboard or a small social media profile picture.

Seek Professional Design Help: If you have the

resources, consider hiring a professional graphic designer or a design agency to create your logo. They have the expertise and knowledge to create a visually appealing and impactful design that aligns with your brand identity. If you prefer a DIY approach, there are also user-friendly design tools available that can assist you in creating a polished logo.

Remember, developing a brand name and designing a logo are essential steps in establishing a strong brand identity. Take the time to research, brainstorm, and iterate to ensure that your brand name resonates with your target audience and your logo captures the essence of your brand. By investing in these key elements, you can create a memorable and recognizable brand that stands out in the market.

Example:

Developing a Brand Name:

Apple Inc. is a prime example of a brand name that resonates with its target audience. The name "Apple" was chosen by the company's co-founder, Steve Jobs, who was inspired by his time working on an apple orchard and his interest in healthy eating. The name "Apple" is simple, memorable, and reflects the brand's values of simplicity, innovation, and user-friendliness. It also aligns with the company's initial focus on personal computers, symbolizing knowledge and education (as in the story of Isaac Newton and the falling apple).

Designing a Logo:

Apple's logo, the iconic bitten apple, is instantly recognizable worldwide. Created by Rob Janoff in 1977, the logo has evolved over time but has retained its core elements. The logo features a simple, silhouette-style apple with a bite taken out of it. The bite serves a dual purpose: it adds a touch of playfulness to the logo and prevents the apple from being mistaken for a cherry. The design is minimalist, timeless, and scalable, making it easily adaptable to various mediums.

The logo's color has changed throughout the years, starting with a rainbow palette in the early days and transitioning to a monochrome design in recent iterations. The sleek, monochrome apple logo represents elegance, sophistication, and innovation, while the vibrant rainbow colors from the early logo represented diversity and creativity.

Apple's logo design is versatile, appearing on their products, packaging, advertising campaigns, and retail stores. Its simplicity and recognizability have made it one of the most iconic and successful logos in the world, cementing Apple's brand identity and creating a strong emotional connection with its target audience.

Overall, Apple's brand name and logo exemplify the importance of developing a brand identity that resonates with the target audience. The simplicity, authenticity, and visual appeal of the brand name and logo have contributed to Apple's success in establishing a strong brand presence and building a loyal customer base.

Chapter 5: Crafting Your Brand Story

What we will be covering in this chapter:

- Telling a compelling narrative that connects with your customers
- Communicating your brand's history, values, and vision

Telling a compelling narrative that connects with your customers is a powerful tool for building brand loyalty and creating a lasting impression. By effectively communicating your brand's history, values, and vision, you can engage your target audience on a deeper level and forge meaningful connections. In this article, we will explore the importance of storytelling in brand communication and provide strategies to craft a compelling narrative that resonates with your customers.

The Power of Storytelling:

Humans have been telling stories since the beginning of time. Stories have the ability to captivate our attention, evoke emotions, and create memorable experiences. When it comes to brand communication, storytelling enables you to present your brand in a way that goes beyond mere product features and benefits. It allows you to create an emotional connection with your audience, making your brand more relatable, authentic, and memorable.

Understanding Your Brand's History:

Every brand has a unique history that has shaped its identity. By sharing your brand's history, you provide customers with a glimpse into its origins, growth, and evolution. This helps establish credibility and builds trust, as customers appreciate knowing the journey your brand has taken to reach its current state. Highlight key milestones, challenges overcome, and significant moments that define your brand's identity. Emphasize how these experiences have shaped your brand's values and vision.

Communicating Your Brand's Values:

Values are the guiding principles that define your brand's behavior and decision-making. Effectively communicating your brand's values is crucial for attracting customers who share those values and establishing long-term relationships. Consider the core principles that drive your brand, such as sustainability, innovation, social responsibility, or customer-centricity. Craft a narrative that demonstrates how your brand's values align with those of your target audience. Showcase real-life examples of how your brand has lived up to its values, whether through community initiatives, ethical sourcing, or philanthropic efforts.

Articulating Your Brand's Vision:

A brand's vision represents its aspirations and long-term goals. It paints a picture of what your brand seeks to achieve and the impact it wants to make in the world. When communicating your brand's vision, focus on the future and the positive change your brand aims to create. Outline the larger purpose behind your products or services and how they contribute to a better world. Customers are often drawn to brands that inspire them and give them a sense of purpose. By articulating your brand's vision, you invite your customers to be a part of that journey.

Crafting a Compelling Narrative:

To tell a compelling brand narrative, it's important to consider the following elements:

a) Authenticity: Be genuine and true to your brand's identity. Customers appreciate authenticity and can sense when a brand is being disingenuous.

b) Emotion: Appeal to the emotions of your audience by tapping into their values, aspirations, and desires. Craft a narrative that evokes feelings and connects on a deeper level.

c) Simplicity: Keep your story simple and easy to understand. Avoid jargon and complex language. Use relatable characters, relatable scenarios, and straightforward storytelling techniques.

d) Consistency: Ensure that your brand narrative is consistent across all channels and touchpoints. Consistency reinforces your brand's identity and makes it easier for customers to recognize and engage with your story.

e) Visuals: Enhance your narrative with visually compelling elements. Utilize images, videos, and design elements that complement your story and create a cohesive brand experience.

f) Customer Engagement: Invite your customers

to be a part of your brand narrative. Encourage them to share their own stories, experiences, and perspectives related to your brand. User-generated content can amplify your narrative and strengthen the bond between your brand and its customers.

In conclusion, storytelling plays a vital role in communicating your brand's history, values, and vision. By crafting a compelling narrative that resonates with your customers, you can forge a deeper connection, build brand loyalty, and differentiate yourself in a crowded marketplace. Remember to be authentic, tap into emotions, keep it simple, stay consistent, incorporate visuals, and engage your customers throughout the storytelling process.

Example:

One real-life example of a brand that successfully sells through storytelling is Coca-Cola. Coca-Cola has been known for its captivating and emotionally-driven storytelling campaigns for many years. They consistently use narratives to create a connection with their consumers and evoke positive emotions tied to their brand.

One notable campaign by Coca-Cola is the "Share a Coke" campaign, which was launched in various countries worldwide. This campaign replaced the Coca-Cola logo on their bottles and cans with popular names, encouraging people to share a Coke with friends and loved ones. The story behind this campaign was to celebrate personal connections and the joy of sharing a special moment with someone. By personalizing their product and tapping into the universal desire for human connection, Coca-Cola created a compelling narrative that resonated with consumers.

Another example is Coca-Cola's iconic Christmas campaigns. Every year, Coca-Cola releases heartwarming and nostalgic advertisements centered around the theme of the holiday season. These ads often feature the well-known Coca-Cola truck and Santa Claus, emphasizing the joy, togetherness, and festive spirit associated with Christmas. By leveraging the power of storytelling, Coca-Cola has created a strong emotional connection with their audience, positioning their brand as an essential part of the holiday tradition.

Through these storytelling campaigns, Coca-Cola has been able to reinforce its brand image as a provider of happiness, joy, and shared experiences. By tapping into universal human emotions and values, they have successfully built a loyal customer base and maintained their position as one of the world's most recognizable and beloved brands.

6

Chapter 6: Developing a Consistent Brand Voice

What we will be covering in this chapter:

- Defining your brand's tone and personality
- Ensuring consistency across all communication channels

Defining your brand's tone and personality and ensuring consistency across all communication channels are crucial aspects of effective brand management. They help establish a strong and memorable brand identity, foster customer trust and loyalty, and differentiate your brand from competitors. In this article, we will delve into the importance of defining your brand's tone and personality and provide strategies for maintaining consistency across various communication channels.

Understanding Brand Tone and Personality:

Your brand's tone refers to the emotional quality and style of communication you use to engage with your audience. It sets the overall atmosphere and mood of your brand's messages. On the other hand, brand personality defines the human traits and characteristics attributed to your brand. It's how your brand is perceived and relates to consumers. Together, they create a distinct voice for your brand.

Importance of Defining Brand Tone and Personality:

a. Building Emotional Connection: A consistent tone and personality help you connect with your target audience on an emotional level. When your brand voice aligns with your customers' values, interests, and aspirations, it creates a sense of relatability, fostering trust and loyalty.

b. Differentiation: In a competitive market, having a unique brand identity is crucial. A well-defined tone and personality set your brand apart from competitors by showcasing its distinctive qualities and values.

c. Brand Consistency: A consistent brand voice

strengthens brand recognition and recall. When your customers encounter consistent messaging across various touchpoints, it reinforces your brand identity and reinforces trust.

Steps to Define Your Brand's Tone and Personality:

a. Understand Your Target Audience: To create an effective brand voice, you need to understand your target audience's demographics, psychographics, preferences, and values. This knowledge will help you tailor your tone and personality to resonate with your audience.

b. Define Core Brand Values: Identify the core values that underpin your brand. These values should guide your messaging and communication strategies. For example, if your brand values authenticity, your tone should be genuine and transparent.

c. Develop Brand Archetypes: Brand archetypes are symbolic characters that represent specific traits and values. They provide a framework for defining your brand's personality. Examples of archetypes include the Hero, the Sage, or the Rebel. Choose the archetype(s) that best align with your brand's identity.

d. Craft a Brand Voice Guide: Document your brand's tone and personality guidelines in a brand voice guide. Include specific language usage, vocabulary, grammar style, and examples of how to apply the brand voice across different communication channels.

Ensuring Consistency Across Communication Channels:

a. Create Communication Guidelines: Establish guidelines that outline how your brand voice should be expressed across various communication channels such as social media, website, emails, advertisements, and customer support. Consistency in tone, messaging, and visual elements is crucial for maintaining a unified brand image.

b. Train and Educate Employees: Ensure that your employees, especially those involved in customer-facing roles, are familiar with your brand voice guidelines. Conduct training sessions or provide resources to help them understand and embody the brand personality consistently.

c. Use Branding Tools: Develop branding tools such as templates, style guides, and visual assets that align with your brand voice. This ensures consistency in design elements, color schemes, typography, and imagery across all communication channels.

d. Monitor and Adapt: Regularly monitor your brand's communication channels to ensure compliance with your brand voice guidelines. Gather feedback from customers, analyze data, and make necessary adjustments to maintain relevance and effectiveness.

Evolving with Your Audience:
As your brand grows and your target audience evolves, periodically review and refine your brand voice. Stay attuned to changes in consumer preferences, cultural trends, and market dynamics. By adapting your tone and personality while staying true to your core values, you can ensure your brand remains relevant and resonates with your audience.

In conclusion, defining your brand's tone and personality and maintaining consistency across all communication channels are integral to successful brand management. They enable you to build emotional connections, differentiate your brand, and enhance brand recognition. By following the steps outlined in this article, you can create a compelling brand voice that resonates with your audience and fosters long-term brand loyalty.

Chapter 7: Building a Strong Online Presence

W hat we will be covering in this chapter:

- Creating a user-friendly and visually appealing website
- Utilizing social media platforms effectively

Creating a User-Friendly and Visually Appealing Website

A user-friendly and visually appealing website is essential for attracting and engaging visitors, increasing conversions, and enhancing the overall user experience. When designing a website, it's important to consider both functionality and aesthetics. Here are some key steps to create a user-friendly and visually appealing website:

Plan the User Experience (UX): Start by defining the target audience and their needs. Consider the user's journey through the website and create a logical and intuitive navigation structure. Use wireframes or mockups to visualize the layout and organization of content.

Responsive Design: With the increasing use of mobile devices, it's crucial to ensure your website is responsive. Responsive design ensures that the website adapts to different screen sizes, providing a seamless experience across desktops, tablets, and smartphones.

Simple and Intuitive Navigation: Make it easy for users to find information on your website. Use clear and concise navigation menus, preferably placed at the top or side of the page. Include a search bar to enable users to quickly find specific content.

Consistent and Clear Visual Hierarchy: Establish a clear visual hierarchy to guide users through your website. Use headings, subheadings, and font styles to differentiate between different levels of information. Highlight important elements using colors, sizes, or spacing to draw attention.

Readable Typography: Select fonts that are legible and easy to read. Avoid using too many different fonts and stick to a maximum of two or three font families. Consider font size, line spacing, and contrast to enhance readability, especially for longer blocks of text.

Use White Space Effectively: White space, also known as negative space, helps in creating a clean and uncluttered design. Properly utilized white space improves readability, highlights important elements, and provides a sense of balance and breathing room.

Color Palette and Visual Branding: Choose a color palette that aligns with your brand identity and conveys the desired emotions. Use colors strategically to create visual interest and guide users' attention. Ensure sufficient contrast between text and background for readability.

High-Quality Imagery and Media: Incorporate high-resolution images and multimedia elements that are relevant to your content. Avoid using generic stock photos and opt for custom photography or illustrations when possible. Optimize image sizes to ensure fast loading times.

Consistent Branding: Maintain consistent branding elements throughout the website. Use the same logo, fonts, colors, and visual styles across all pages to reinforce brand recognition and create a cohesive experience.

Optimize Page Load Speed: Slow-loading websites lead to higher bounce rates. Compress images, minify code, and utilize caching techniques to optimize page load speed. Test the website's performance regularly and make necessary optimizations.

Clear Call-to-Action (CTA): Guide users towards desired actions by using clear and compelling CTAs. Use contrasting colors, bold typography, and positioning to make CTAs stand out. Make sure they are placed strategically and relevant to the content on the page.

User-Friendly Forms: If your website includes forms, make them user-friendly by keeping them concise and easy to fill out. Use tooltips or placeholders to provide guidance, and avoid unnecessary fields. Implement validation to ensure accurate data entry.

Utilizing Social Media Platforms Effectively

In today's digital age, social media platforms offer tremendous opportunities to connect with your target audience, increase brand visibility, and drive traffic to your website. To utilize social media effectively, consider the following strategies:

Define Your Goals: Clearly define your goals for social media marketing. Is it to increase brand awareness, drive website traffic, generate leads, or engage with your audience? Having specific goals will help you measure the effectiveness of your efforts.

Choose the Right Platforms: Identify the social media platforms that align with your target audience and industry. Each platform has its own unique user base and features, so focus on the ones where your audience is most active.

Consistent Branding: Maintain consistent branding across all social media platforms. Use the same profile picture, cover photo, and bio information. Consistency builds brand recognition and establishes a cohesive presence.

Engage with Your Audience: Social media is a two-way communication channel. Respond to comments, messages, and mentions promptly. Engage with your audience by asking questions, running polls, and encouraging discussions.

Quality Content Creation: Share high-quality and valuable content that resonates with your target audience. Use a mix of formats like text, images, videos, and infographics. Create a content calendar to plan and schedule posts in advance.

Visual Appeal: Incorporate visually appealing graphics and media in your social media posts. Use eye-catching images, well-designed templates, and branded elements to capture attention and encourage engagement.

Hashtags and Keywords: Research and use relevant hashtags and keywords in your social media posts. This helps increase the discoverability of your content and reach a wider audience interested in your niche.

Paid Advertising: Consider using paid advertising options provided by social media platforms. Target your ads based on demographics, interests, and behaviors to reach your ideal audience. Monitor and optimize your ad campaigns for maximum results.

Influencer Partnerships: Collaborate with influencers or industry experts who have a significant following and influence. This can help expand your reach, build credibility, and tap into their engaged audience.

Analytics and Insights: Utilize the analytics and insights provided by social media platforms to track the performance of your posts and campaigns. Analyze the data to understand what content resonates with your audience and adjust your strategies accordingly.

Community Building: Foster a sense of community on your social media platforms. Encourage user-generated content, run contests or giveaways, and feature customer testimonials. This helps in building brand loyalty and advocacy.

Stay Updated: Social media platforms are constantly evolving. Stay updated with the latest trends, features, and best practices. Experiment with new formats, tools, and strategies to keep your social media presence fresh and engaging.

By following these guidelines, you can create a user-friendly and visually appealing website that provides a seamless experience for your visitors.

Additionally, effectively utilizing social media platforms can help you connect with your audience, build brand awareness, and drive traffic to your website. Remember to continuously monitor and adapt your strategies to stay ahead in the ever-changing digital landscape.

Example:
User-Friendly and Visually Appealing Website:

Garden Oasis understands that their target audience consists of both novice and experienced gardeners who visit their website for product information, gardening tips, and to schedule landscaping services. They start by planning the user experience, ensuring easy navigation and a logical flow of information.

The website employs responsive design, ensuring it looks great and functions well on various devices. The navigation menu is clear and intuitive, featuring categories like "Products," "Landscaping Services," and "Gardening Tips." They also include a search bar for users to quickly find specific products or articles.

Garden Oasis maintains a consistent visual hierarchy, using headings and subheadings to organize content. They utilize a readable typography that complements their brand image. The color palette consists of earthy tones and vibrant greens, reflecting the company's connection to nature.

The website incorporates high-quality imagery showcasing beautiful gardens, along with product photos and illustrations. They use white space effectively, giving the content room to breathe and creating a clean and uncluttered design.

Clear call-to-action buttons are strategically placed throughout the website, guiding users to purchase products, book services, or subscribe to their newsletter. User-friendly forms are employed for requesting landscaping quotes or signing up for workshops, keeping them concise and easy to fill out.

Utilizing Social Media Platforms Effectively:
Garden Oasis identifies that their target audience actively engages on social media platforms like Facebook, Instagram, and Pinterest. They develop a social media strategy aligned with their goals.

Garden Oasis creates consistent branding across their social media profiles, using their logo, brand colors, and consistent messaging. They share visually appealing posts that showcase their products, before-and-after landscaping transformations, gardening tips, and DIY tutorials.

They engage with their audience by promptly responding to comments, messages, and mentions. They ask questions, encourage users to share their gardening experiences, and run polls to foster discussions. They also encourage user-generated content by featuring customer garden photos and testimonials.

Garden Oasis utilizes relevant hashtags and keywords in their social media posts to increase discoverability. They run targeted ad campaigns on social media platforms, reaching people interested in gardening and landscaping within their local area.

Influencer partnerships are formed with popular gardening bloggers and local landscapers who have a significant social media following. These influencers create sponsored content, showcasing Garden Oasis products and services to their engaged audience, helping to increase brand reach and credibility.

Garden Oasis monitors social media analytics and insights to understand what content performs best.

They analyze engagement rates, reach, and click-through rates to refine their content strategy. They adapt to new trends and features, such as creating video tutorials or live gardening sessions to keep their social media presence fresh and engaging.

By implementing these strategies, Garden Oasis successfully creates a user-friendly and visually appealing website, providing an enjoyable experience for their visitors. They effectively utilize social media platforms to connect with their audience, increase brand awareness, and drive traffic to their website, ultimately leading to increased sales and customer loyalty.

8

Chapter 8: Leveraging Content Marketing

W hat we will be covering in this chapter:

- Developing a content strategy that aligns with your brand
- Creating valuable and engaging content for your audience

Developing a content strategy that aligns with your brand is crucial for establishing a strong online presence and effectively reaching your target audience. It involves creating a plan that outlines your brand's objectives, target audience, key messages, and the types of content you will create to engage and provide value to your audience. Here are some steps to develop a content strategy that aligns with your brand:

Define your brand: Start by clearly defining your brand's mission, values, and unique selling proposition. Understand what sets your brand apart from competitors and how you want to be perceived by your target audience. This will serve as the foundation for your content strategy.

Identify your target audience: Determine who your target audience is, their demographics, interests, and needs. Conduct market research, analyze customer data, and create buyer personas to gain insights into your audience's preferences and behaviors. Understanding your audience will help you create content that resonates with them.

Set content objectives: Establish clear objectives for your content strategy. Do you want to increase brand awareness, drive website traffic, generate leads, or establish thought leadership? Align your content objectives with your overall business goals to ensure they contribute to your brand's growth.

Conduct a content audit: Evaluate your existing content to identify strengths, weaknesses, and gaps. Determine what type of content has performed well in the past, what topics resonate with your audience, and which channels have been most effective. This audit will help you understand what content to leverage and what areas need improvement.

Determine content types and formats: Based on your brand's objectives and target audience preferences, decide on the types of content you will create. This may include blog posts, videos, podcasts, social media posts, infographics, case studies, whitepapers, or webinars. Consider which formats are most suitable for delivering your message and engaging your audience effectively.

Create a content calendar: Develop a content calendar that outlines the topics, formats, and publishing schedule for your content. This will help you stay organized and consistent in delivering valuable content to your audience. Align your content calendar with key events, product launches, and industry trends to stay relevant.

Craft compelling and valuable content: When creating content, focus on providing value to your audience. Address their pain points, answer their questions, and offer solutions to their problems. Use a mix of educational, informative, and entertaining content that aligns with your brand's voice and values. Maintain consistency in tone, style, and messaging across all your content.

Optimize for SEO: Incorporate search engine optimization (SEO) strategies into your content to improve its visibility and reach. Conduct keyword research to identify relevant keywords and incorporate them naturally into your content. Optimize meta tags, headings, and image alt tags. Ensure your content is easily discoverable by search engines and resonates with your target audience.

Promote and distribute your content: Develop a promotion and distribution plan to ensure your content reaches your target audience. Utilize social media platforms, email marketing, influencer collaborations, guest posting, and paid advertising to amplify your content's reach. Engage with your audience through comments, shares, and discussions to foster a sense of community.

Measure and analyze results: Regularly track and analyze the performance of your content. Monitor metrics such as website traffic, engagement, social media reach, conversions, and lead generation. Identify what content is resonating with your audience and adjust your strategy accordingly. Use analytics tools to gain insights into audience behavior and preferences.

By developing a content strategy that aligns with

your brand, you can effectively engage and provide value to your audience. Continuously evaluate and refine your strategy based on audience feedback and changing trends to maintain relevance and drive your brand's success.

Example:

Let's consider a fitness apparel brand targeting fitness enthusiasts and individuals interested in leading a healthy lifestyle. The brand's content strategy focuses on providing valuable information, inspiration, and promoting their products. Here's how they can create engaging content:

Educational blog posts: The brand can create blog posts that provide fitness tips, workout routines, nutrition advice, and information about the latest trends in the fitness industry. For example, they can publish an article titled "5 Effective Workout Routines for Building Lean Muscle" or "The Ultimate Guide to Healthy Meal Prep." These blog posts would offer practical information and advice to their audience, helping them achieve their fitness goals.

Video tutorials: To engage their audience visually, the brand can create video tutorials demonstrating proper exercise form, workout routines, or healthy recipes. They can collaborate with fitness trainers or influencers to showcase different workout variations or provide expert advice. These videos would not only educate their audience but also motivate and inspire them to lead an active lifestyle.

Inspirational success stories: The brand can share success stories of individuals who have achieved their fitness goals using their products or following their advice. They can interview customers who have experienced significant weight loss, improved strength, or overcome health challenges. By sharing these stories, the brand inspires their audience, establishes credibility, and showcases the transformative power of their products.

Social media challenges: The brand can create social media challenges that encourage their followers to participate and share their progress. For example, they can initiate a "30-day fitness challenge" where participants perform specific exercises or follow a workout plan. By sharing their journey using a branded hashtag, participants engage with the brand and each other, fostering a sense of community and accountability.

Interactive quizzes and polls: To make their content

more interactive, the brand can create quizzes and polls related to fitness, nutrition, or wellness topics. For instance, they can create a quiz titled "What's Your Fitness Personality?" or a poll asking their audience to vote on their favorite healthy snack. These interactive elements not only engage the audience but also provide insights into their preferences and interests.

Product demonstrations and reviews: The brand can create content that showcases their products in action. They can create videos or blog posts featuring athletes or fitness influencers using their apparel during workouts or outdoor activities. Additionally, they can collaborate with influencers to review their products, providing honest feedback and recommendations to their audience.

User-generated content: Encouraging their audience to create and share content featuring their products can be a powerful engagement strategy. The brand can run contests or campaigns where participants submit photos or videos of themselves using their products. By featuring user-generated content on their social media channels or website, the brand not only engages their audience but also creates a sense of community and authenticity.

Expert interviews and guest posts: Collaborating with fitness experts, nutritionists, or trainers to provide expert insights can add value to the brand's content. They can conduct interviews or invite guest bloggers to share their knowledge and expertise. This variety of perspectives helps establish the brand as a reliable source of information and demonstrates their commitment to providing valuable content to their audience.

By consistently creating valuable and engaging content like educational blog posts, video tutorials, success stories, interactive challenges, and expert collaborations, the fitness apparel brand can connect with their target audience on a deeper level. This content strategy not only provides value to their audience but also strengthens their brand positioning and drives customer loyalty.

Chapter 9: Building Brand Trust and Credibility

What we will be covering in this chapter:

- Establishing trust through excellent customer service
- Implementing transparency and ethical practices

Establishing trust through excellent customer service:

Establishing trust is crucial for any business to thrive and build long-term relationships with its customers. One of the most effective ways to establish trust is through excellent customer service. When customers feel valued, heard, and supported by a company, they are more likely to trust that company and continue doing business with them. Here's an elaboration on how excellent customer service can contribute to trust-building:

Responsive communication: Promptly addressing customer inquiries, concerns, and feedback demonstrates that the company values its customers and is committed to providing satisfactory solutions. This open and transparent communication builds trust by showing that the company is attentive and dedicated to resolving any issues that may arise.

Personalization: Treating customers as individuals and tailoring interactions to their specific needs and preferences can greatly enhance trust. Personalization can be achieved by remembering customer details, past purchases, or preferences, which showcases a commitment to building a relationship and delivering a personalized experience.

Consistency and reliability: Delivering consistent and reliable service is crucial for building trust. When customers have consistent experiences that align with their expectations, they develop a sense of reliability and trust in the company's ability to consistently meet their needs.

Empathy and understanding: Demonstrating empathy and understanding towards customers' concerns and challenges fosters trust. By showing genuine care and providing empathetic support, companies can create a positive emotional connection with their customers, leading to increased trust and loyalty.

Going the extra mile: Exceeding customer expectations by going above and beyond can make a significant impact on trust-building. Whether it's offering proactive assistance, providing additional resources, or surprising customers with unexpected perks or benefits, these actions demonstrate a company's commitment to customer satisfaction and help solidify trust.

Implementing transparency and ethical practices:

Transparency and ethical practices are fundamental to establishing trust with customers, employees, and the broader community. In today's business landscape, consumers are increasingly concerned about how companies operate, their impact on society, and the values they uphold. Implementing transparency and ethical practices not only strengthens trust but also contributes to long-term success. Here's an elaboration on the importance of transparency and ethical practices:

Clear communication: Transparency begins with clear and honest communication. Companies should provide accurate and comprehensive information about their products, services, pricing, policies, and any potential risks. Clear communication ensures that customers are well-informed and helps prevent misunderstandings or deceptive practices.

Ethical sourcing and production: Adopting ethical practices throughout the supply chain, from sourcing raw materials to manufacturing, is essential. This includes ensuring fair labor practices, promoting environmental sustainability, and avoiding unethical practices such as child labor, exploitation, or environmental harm. Ethical sourcing and production practices not only build trust but also contribute to a positive brand image.

Privacy and data protection: Respecting customer privacy and protecting their personal data is paramount. Implementing robust security measures, obtaining informed consent for data collection and usage, and being transparent about how customer data is handled are crucial elements of building trust in the digital age.

Social and environmental responsibility: Demonstrating a commitment to social and environmental responsibility can significantly enhance trust. This involves actively supporting causes, engaging in philanthropy, reducing environmental impact, and contributing positively to the community. By aligning with customers' values and actively addressing social and environmental challenges, companies can build trust and loyalty.

Accountability and integrity: Upholding high standards of accountability and integrity is vital for building trust. Companies should take responsibility for their actions, promptly address any mistakes or issues, and maintain a culture of ethical conduct throughout the organization. By being transparent about their decision-making processes and taking accountability when necessary, companies can earn and maintain trust.

In summary, establishing trust through excellent customer service and implementing transparency and ethical practices are critical for businesses to thrive in today's competitive landscape. By prioritizing these principles, companies can build long-term relationships with customers, enhance their brand reputation, and contribute to a sustainable and ethical business environment.

10

Chapter 10: Engaging with Your Customers

W hat we will be covering in this chapter:

- Cultivating a strong customer relationship management strategy
- Encouraging customer feedback and addressing concerns

Cultivating a strong customer relationship management (CRM) strategy is crucial for businesses looking to build long-term relationships with their customers. It involves implementing various practices and processes to effectively manage interactions, improve customer satisfaction, and drive customer loyalty. Here are some key aspects to consider when cultivating a strong CRM strategy:

Data collection and analysis: One of the foundations of a successful CRM strategy is the collection and analysis of customer data. This includes gathering information such as customer preferences, purchase history, communication preferences, and feedback. By analyzing this data, businesses can gain insights into customer behavior and preferences, allowing them to tailor their offerings and communication to better serve their customers.

Personalization and segmentation: A strong CRM strategy involves personalizing customer experiences and segmenting customers based on their specific needs and preferences. By leveraging the collected data, businesses can deliver targeted marketing messages, recommendations, and offers, making customers feel valued and understood.

Effective communication channels: To build strong relationships, it's important to establish effective communication channels with customers. This includes providing multiple channels such as email, phone, social media, and live chat, enabling customers to reach out and engage with the business in a way that suits them best. Prompt and personalized responses are crucial in nurturing customer relationships and addressing their concerns.

Proactive customer support: A proactive approach to customer support is vital for cultivating strong relationships. Encouraging customers to provide feedback and addressing their concerns promptly and effectively demonstrates that their opinions and experiences are valued. By actively seeking feedback, businesses can identify areas for improvement, enhance their products or services, and foster trust and loyalty among customers.

Loyalty programs and rewards: Implementing loyalty programs and rewards can be an effective strategy to cultivate strong customer relationships. These programs can incentivize customers to stay engaged with the brand, make repeat purchases, and refer others. By acknowledging and rewarding customer loyalty, businesses can reinforce positive relationships and encourage customers to become brand advocates.

Continuous improvement: A strong CRM strategy is a dynamic process that requires continuous improvement. Regularly reviewing and analyzing customer feedback, monitoring customer satisfaction metrics, and adapting strategies accordingly are essential. This iterative approach helps businesses stay responsive to customer needs and preferences, fostering long-term relationships.

In summary, cultivating a strong CRM strategy involves collecting and analyzing customer data, personalizing customer experiences, establishing effective communication channels, providing proactive customer support, implementing loyalty programs, and continuously improving based on customer feedback. By prioritizing these aspects, businesses can build and maintain strong customer relationships, leading to increased customer satisfaction, loyalty, and ultimately, business growth.

Example of a CRM Strategy for a Fictional Retail solution:

Data Collection and Analysis:
Implement a robust CRM system to collect and store customer data, including demographics, purchase history, browsing behavior, and communication preferences.

Analyze the collected data to identify patterns, trends, and customer preferences, enabling personalized marketing and communication strategies.

Personalization and Segmentation:
Segment customers based on their demographics, preferences, and purchase behavior to create targeted marketing campaigns and personalized product recommendations.

Utilize automation tools to deliver personalized emails, product suggestions, and offers to specific customer segments.

Effective Communication Channels:
Provide multiple communication channels such as email, phone, live chat, and social media platforms, ensuring customers can easily reach out for support or inquiries.

Develop a self-service portal where customers can find answers to common queries and access resources such as FAQs, tutorials, and product guides.

Proactive Customer Support:
Encourage customers to provide feedback through surveys, reviews, and ratings, and promptly address their concerns or complaints.

Implement a ticketing system to track and resolve customer issues efficiently, ensuring timely responses and resolutions.

Loyalty Programs and Rewards:
Create a customer loyalty program that offers incentives, rewards, and exclusive benefits to encourage repeat purchases and brand advocacy.

Establish a referral program to reward customers who refer new customers to the business.

Continuous Improvement:

Regularly monitor customer satisfaction metrics, such as Net Promoter Score (NPS) or Customer Satisfaction (CSAT), to gauge customer sentiment and identify areas for improvement.

Leverage customer feedback and data analysis to refine products, services, and customer experiences, ensuring ongoing enhancement and innovation.

Integration and Collaboration:

Integrate the CRM system with other business tools, such as marketing automation platforms, e-commerce platforms, and customer support software, to streamline processes and ensure a seamless customer experience.

Foster collaboration and communication between different departments, such as marketing, sales, and customer support, to share customer insights and align strategies.

Training and Development:

Invest in training programs for employees to enhance their customer service and relationship management skills.

Foster a customer-centric culture throughout the organization, emphasizing the importance of building strong customer relationships.

Example of a CRM strategy for a SAAS company:

Customer data collection: The first step is to collect relevant customer data, such as user profiles, subscription information, usage patterns, and support interactions. This can be achieved through in-app analytics, registration forms, surveys, and integration with customer support systems.

Segmentation and personalization: Utilize the collected data to segment customers based on their usage patterns, industry, company size, or any other relevant criteria. This segmentation allows for targeted and personalized communication, such as sending tailored product recommendations, educational content, or feature updates that are most relevant to each customer segment.

Proactive onboarding and training: Implement a robust onboarding process to guide new customers through their initial setup and familiarize them with the software's features and benefits. Offer resources like tutorials, webinars, and documentation to help them maximize the value of your product. Provide proactive support during the onboarding phase to ensure a smooth transition and address any questions or concerns.

Regular communication and engagement: Stay in touch with customers through regular communication channels like email newsletters, blog updates, and social media engagement. Share product updates, industry insights, and best practices to keep customers informed and engaged. Leverage marketing automation tools to send targeted messages based on customer behavior and preferences.

Customer feedback and support: Encourage customers to provide feedback through surveys, feedback forms, or in-app feedback mechanisms. Actively listen to their concerns and suggestions and address them promptly. Implement a robust ticketing system or customer support software to manage and resolve customer issues efficiently, ensuring timely and satisfactory resolutions.

Upselling and cross-selling: Identify opportunities to upsell or cross-sell additional features, modules, or subscription tiers to existing customers. Leverage customer usage data and behavior to identify potential upsell opportunities and proactively present relevant offers. Provide personalized recommendations based on their specific needs and usage patterns to drive expansion revenue.

Customer success and advocacy: Develop a customer success program to ensure customers achieve their desired outcomes with your software. Assign dedicated customer success managers to help customers set goals, monitor progress, and provide ongoing support. Encourage satisfied customers to become advocates by offering referral programs, case studies, and testimonials that highlight their success stories.

Continuous improvement and analysis: Regularly analyze customer data, usage metrics, and feedback to identify areas for improvement. Use this information to iterate and enhance the product, address pain points, and optimize the customer experience. Incorporate customer feedback into product roadmaps and prioritize feature development based on customer needs and preferences.

Remember, every CRM strategy should be tailored to the specific needs and goals of the SaaS company. This example provides a general framework that can be customized and expanded upon based on the company's unique offerings, target audience, and business objectives.

11

Chapter 11: Leveraging Influencer Marketing

W hat we will be covering in this chapter:

- Collaborating with influencers to increase brand visibility
- Identifying the right influencers for your target audience

Collaborating with influencers has become an increasingly popular marketing strategy for businesses to increase their brand visibility and reach a wider audience. Influencers, who are individuals with a dedicated following on social media platforms, have the ability to impact the purchasing decisions of their followers through their recommendations and endorsements.

To effectively collaborate with influencers and maximize the benefits of such partnerships, it is crucial to identify the right influencers for your target audience. Here are some key steps to consider:

Define your target audience: Before identifying influencers, you need to have a clear understanding of your target audience. Consider factors such as demographics, interests, and values of your ideal customers. This information will help you narrow down the pool of potential influencers who align with your brand and can effectively engage your target audience.

Conduct thorough research: Once you have a clear understanding of your target audience, begin researching influencers who have a strong presence within that audience segment. Explore various social media platforms such as Instagram, YouTube, TikTok, and blogs to find influencers who create content relevant to your industry or niche. Look for influencers who have an engaged and active following, as well as a track record of producing high-quality content.

Evaluate influencer credibility and authenticity: It's important to assess the credibility and authenticity of influencers before collaborating with them.

Review their content, engagement metrics, and feedback from their followers. Pay attention to the authenticity of their brand partnerships and how well they integrate sponsored content into their overall brand image. Ensure that the influencer's values align with your brand's values to maintain a genuine connection with your target audience.

Analyze engagement metrics: Assess the engagement metrics of potential influencers to gauge their effectiveness in driving audience interaction and impact. Look for metrics such as likes, comments, shares, and views to determine the level of engagement their content generates. Quality engagement indicates that the influencer has an active and loyal audience that is receptive to their recommendations.

Consider reach and relevance: While considering influencers, it's essential to strike a balance between reach and relevance. Larger influencers may have a broader reach, but smaller influencers often have a more engaged and niche audience. Depending on your marketing goals and budget, you may choose to collaborate with a mix of macro-influencers (those with a large following) and micro-influencers (those with a smaller following but strong influence within a specific community).

Reach out and establish a connection: Once you have identified potential influencers, reach out to them with a personalized message explaining why you believe they would be a good fit for your brand. Express your admiration for their work and highlight how your collaboration can be mutually beneficial. Offer a clear outline of what you expect from the partnership and discuss any compensation or incentives you can provide.

Monitor and measure results: After establishing collaborations with influencers, monitor the performance of your campaigns closely. Track key performance indicators (KPIs) such as website traffic, conversions, and social media engagement to assess the effectiveness of the partnership. Use these insights to refine your influencer marketing strategy and build long-term relationships with influencers who consistently deliver positive results.

Remember, the key to successful influencer collaborations lies in finding influencers who can authentically represent your brand and resonate with your target audience. By investing time and effort into identifying the right influencers, you can increase brand visibility, generate awareness, and drive meaningful engagement with your target market.

Example:

1. Defining the target audience: The beauty brand determines that their target audience is predominantly young women aged 18-30 who are interested in makeup trends, skincare, and beauty tips.

2. Conducting research: They start researching popular social media platforms such as Instagram and YouTube to find influencers who cater to the beauty and cosmetics niche. They look for influencers with a strong following of young women who actively engage with their content.

3. Evaluating credibility and authenticity: The brand reviews the content of potential influencers and assesses the authenticity of their brand partnerships. They look for influencers who genuinely use and promote beauty products and whose values align with their own, ensuring that the collaborations will resonate with their target audience.

4. Analyzing engagement metrics: The brand considers influencers with high engagement rates, such as those who receive a significant number of likes, comments, and shares on their posts. They focus on influencers whose content generates meaningful discussions and

interactions within the beauty community.

5. Considering reach and relevance: The brand decides to collaborate with a mix of macro-influencers and micro-influencers. They reach out to macro-influencers with a large following, such as beauty gurus with hundreds of thousands or even millions of followers. They also engage with micro-influencers who have smaller but highly engaged audiences within specific beauty niches, such as skincare or natural makeup.

6. Reaching out and establishing a connection: The brand sends personalized messages to the selected influencers, expressing their admiration for their work and explaining why they believe a collaboration would be mutually beneficial. They outline their expectations for the partnership, such as promoting specific products, creating tutorial videos, or sharing discount codes, and discuss compensation or incentives.

7. Monitoring and measuring results: Once the collaborations are established, the beauty brand closely monitors the performance of each campaign. They track metrics such as website traffic generated by influencer promotions, the number of conversions, and social media engagement. They analyze

the results to assess the effectiveness of each collaboration and make adjustments if necessary.

For example, the beauty brand collaborates with a popular beauty YouTuber who has a strong following of young women interested in makeup tutorials. The YouTuber creates a video showcasing the brand's latest makeup collection and shares her honest review and tutorial on how to use the products. The video generates a significant amount of engagement, with thousands of likes, comments, and shares. As a result, the brand experiences a noticeable increase in website traffic, a surge in product sales, and gains new followers on their social media channels.

By leveraging the influence and reach of relevant influencers, the beauty brand successfully increases its brand visibility among the target audience and establishes a stronger presence within the beauty community.

12

Chapter 12: Creating a Memorable Customer Experience

What we will be covering in this chapter:

- Designing an exceptional customer journey
- Going above and beyond to exceed customer expectations

Designing an exceptional customer journey and going above and beyond to exceed customer expectations are crucial aspects of building strong customer relationships and creating a competitive edge in today's business landscape. By prioritizing these aspects, companies can differentiate themselves from competitors, foster customer loyalty, and drive sustainable growth. This comprehensive guide will delve into the key considerations and strategies involved in designing an exceptional customer journey and exceeding customer expectations.

Understanding Customer Needs and Expectations:

To design a customer journey that exceeds expectations, it is essential to thoroughly understand your customers' needs, expectations, and pain points. This understanding can be gained through market research, customer surveys, feedback channels, and analyzing customer data. By leveraging this information, you can identify the key touchpoints throughout the customer journey and align your strategies accordingly.

Mapping the Customer Journey:

Once you have a clear understanding of your customers' needs and expectations, the next step is to map out the customer journey. This involves visualizing the entire end-to-end experience a customer has with your company, starting from the initial interaction to post-purchase support. By mapping the customer journey, you can identify potential gaps, pain points, and areas of improvement, enabling you to create a more seamless and satisfying experience for your customers.

Personalization and Customization:

Customers today expect personalized experiences tailored to their unique preferences and requirements. By leveraging customer data, such as purchase history, browsing behavior, and demographic information, you can customize the customer journey to create a more relevant and engaging experience. Personalization can manifest in various ways, such as personalized product recommendations, targeted marketing messages, and customized user interfaces. The more you can personalize the customer journey, the more likely you are to exceed customer expectations.

Seamless Omnichannel Experience:

In today's interconnected world, customers interact with businesses through various channels, including websites, mobile apps, social media, physical stores, and customer service hotlines. To provide an exceptional customer journey, it is crucial to ensure a seamless omnichannel experience. This means maintaining consistency in branding, messaging, and user experience across all touchpoints, allowing customers to transition effortlessly between channels without any loss of information or context. A seamless omnichannel experience enhances convenience, reduces friction, and ultimately exceeds customer expectations.

Anticipating Customer Needs:

One way to go above and beyond customer expectations is by proactively anticipating their needs. By leveraging data analytics and customer insights, you can identify patterns and trends that can help you predict what customers might need in the future. For example, if a customer frequently purchases a certain type of product, you can proactively offer replenishment reminders or suggest related products that align with their preferences. By anticipating customer needs, you can demonstrate a deep understanding of your customers and provide proactive solutions, leading to heightened satisfaction and loyalty.

Exceptional Customer Service:

Delivering exceptional customer service is paramount in exceeding customer expectations. This involves investing in well-trained and empathetic customer service representatives who are equipped to handle customer inquiries, complaints, and requests effectively. Prompt response times, active listening, and personalized solutions are key components of exceptional customer service. Additionally, empowering employees to make decisions and resolve issues on the spot can further enhance the customer experience. By providing outstanding customer service, you can create positive emotional connections and foster long-term customer loyalty.

Surprise and Delight:

To truly exceed customer expectations, it's essential to surprise and delight customers at various touchpoints. This can be achieved through unexpected gestures, such as sending personalized thank-you notes, offering exclusive discounts or rewards, providing complimentary upgrades, or hosting special events for loyal customers. Surprise and delight moments create positive memories and emotional connections, leaving a lasting impression that sets your brand apart.

Continuous Improvement and Feedback:

Designing an exceptional customer journey is an ongoing process. It's crucial to regularly gather customer feedback, track key performance metrics, and analyze customer satisfaction levels. This information can help you identify areas for improvement and fine-tune your strategies to consistently exceed customer expectations. Actively seeking and incorporating customer feedback demonstrates your commitment to delivering an exceptional experience and ensures that your customer journey remains relevant and effective over time.

In conclusion, designing an exceptional customer journey and going above and beyond to exceed customer expectations require a deep understanding of customer needs, seamless omnichannel experiences, personalization, exceptional customer service, anticipation of customer needs, surprise and delight moments, and continuous improvement. By prioritizing these elements and consistently striving to exceed expectations, businesses can build strong customer relationships, drive customer loyalty, and ultimately achieve sustainable growth in today's competitive marketplace.

13

Chapter 13: Harnessing the Power of Brand Advocacy

What we will be covering in this chapter:

- Encouraging loyal customers to become brand advocates
- Implementing referral programs and loyalty rewards

Encouraging loyal customers to become brand advocates is a powerful marketing strategy that can significantly boost a company's brand awareness, customer acquisition, and customer retention. When customers become advocates for a brand, they voluntarily spread positive word-of-mouth, recommend products or services to their networks, and essentially become walking advertisements. This form of marketing is highly effective because it harnesses the power of personal relationships and trust, which are crucial factors influencing consumer purchasing decisions.

To encourage loyal customers to become brand advocates, businesses can implement various strategies and initiatives. Two popular methods are implementing referral programs and loyalty rewards. Let's explore each of these strategies in detail:

Referral Programs:
Referral programs are structured systems that incentivize customers to refer friends, family, or colleagues to the brand. Here's how they work:

a. Offer incentives: Provide a compelling incentive for both the advocate and the referred customer. This could be in the form of discounts, freebies, exclusive access to new products, or even monetary rewards.

b. Simple sharing mechanism: Make it easy for advocates to share the brand with others. Provide referral codes, personalized links, or social media sharing buttons that enable seamless sharing across various platforms.

c. Track and reward referrals: Implement a system to track referrals accurately. When a referred customer makes a purchase, reward the advocate promptly with the promised incentive.

   d. Multi-tier rewards: Consider offering escalating rewards for advocates who refer multiple customers. This provides an extra incentive for advocates to continue promoting the brand.

By implementing a referral program, businesses can tap into the existing network of loyal customers and leverage their relationships to acquire new customers. The advocates, in turn, feel valued and rewarded for their support, enhancing their loyalty and further strengthening the relationship with the brand.

Loyalty Rewards:

   Loyalty rewards programs are designed to incentivize and retain loyal customers by offering them exclusive benefits and rewards. Here's how to implement an effective loyalty rewards program:

   a. Define tiers or levels: Create different tiers or levels within the loyalty program, each offering increasing benefits or rewards. This encourages customers to engage more with the brand to unlock higher levels.

   b. Point-based system: Assign points for various actions, such as purchases, social media engagement, referrals, or writing reviews. Customers can accumulate points and redeem them for rewards or discounts.

c. Personalized offers: Tailor rewards and offers based on individual customer preferences and purchase history. Personalization enhances the customer experience and makes them feel valued.

d. Gamification elements: Incorporate gamification elements, such as challenges, badges, or leaderboards, to make the loyalty program more engaging and fun for customers.

e. Special events or promotions: Organize exclusive events or promotions specifically for loyalty program members. This creates a sense of exclusivity and strengthens the bond between the brand and its loyal customers.

Loyalty rewards programs not only incentivize customers to continue purchasing from the brand but also increase customer satisfaction and foster a sense of belonging and community. Satisfied and engaged customers are more likely to become brand advocates, as they genuinely appreciate the brand and its offerings.

In conclusion, encouraging loyal customers to become brand advocates is a valuable marketing strategy. Implementing referral programs and loyalty rewards are effective ways to nurture and harness the advocacy potential of existing customers. By providing incentives, simplifying sharing mechanisms, and personalizing offers, businesses can motivate their loyal customers to become advocates and amplify the brand's reach, credibility, and customer base.

Example:

Dropbox, a cloud storage service, employed a referral program to drive customer acquisition and growth. The program offered existing users and new customers incentives for referring others to sign up for Dropbox. Here's how they executed their strategy:

Incentives: Dropbox offered a "Give a little, get a little" incentive structure. Existing users were rewarded with additional storage space for every successful referral they made, while the referred users received extra storage space as well.

Simple sharing mechanism: Dropbox made it extremely easy for users to share their referral links with others. Users could send invites via email, share on social media platforms, or even generate unique referral links to share manually.

Tracking and rewarding: Dropbox implemented a tracking system that accurately monitored successful referrals. Once a referred user signed up and installed Dropbox, both the advocate and the referred user received additional storage space, fulfilling the promised incentives.

Multi-tier rewards: To further motivate advocates, Dropbox introduced a multi-tier rewards system. Users could earn additional storage space for reaching milestones, such as referring multiple users or engaging with Dropbox's social media accounts.

By implementing this referral program, Dropbox successfully turned its loyal customers into brand advocates. The program leveraged the existing user base to acquire new customers, as satisfied customers enthusiastically referred others to join the service. In return, both the advocate and the referred user received valuable incentives, creating a win-win situation.

Additionally, Dropbox also implemented a loyalty rewards program called Dropbox Pro. Users who upgraded to the paid version of Dropbox received benefits such as increased storage space, advanced sharing features, and priority customer support. This loyalty program aimed to retain existing customers and encourage them to continue using Dropbox's premium services.

The combination of referral programs and loyalty rewards helped Dropbox achieve tremendous growth. By incentivizing their loyal customers to become advocates and rewarding them for their efforts, Dropbox amplified its brand reach and acquired a significant number of new customers. This strategy not only increased customer acquisition but also strengthened customer loyalty and retention.

The success of Dropbox's referral program and loyalty rewards program demonstrates the effectiveness of these strategies in turning loyal customers into brand advocates. By offering valuable incentives, streamlining sharing mechanisms, and providing personalized rewards, Dropbox successfully encouraged its customers to spread positive word-of-mouth and contribute to the company's growth.

Chapter 14: Expanding Your Brand's Reach

What we will be covering in this chapter:

- Exploring strategic partnerships and collaborations
- Expanding into new markets and demographics

Exploring strategic partnerships and collaborations:

Exploring strategic partnerships and collaborations refers to the process of seeking out and forming mutually beneficial relationships with other organizations or individuals in order to achieve strategic objectives. These partnerships and collaborations can take various forms, such as joint ventures, licensing agreements, co-branding initiatives, research and development collaborations, or even mergers and acquisitions.

The primary purpose of exploring strategic partnerships and collaborations is to leverage the complementary strengths and resources of each party involved, thereby creating a synergy that can lead to increased competitiveness, growth, and innovation. By joining forces with another entity, a company can gain access to new markets, technologies, expertise, distribution channels, or customer segments that would be difficult or costly to acquire independently.

There are several key reasons why organizations engage in exploring strategic partnerships and collaborations:

Market expansion: Strategic partnerships allow companies to enter new markets or expand their presence in existing markets more efficiently and effectively. By partnering with local organizations or those with established market access, a company can leverage their knowledge, network, and resources to penetrate new geographies and reach a wider customer base.

Resource sharing: Collaborations enable organizations to pool their resources, whether it's financial capital, intellectual property, manufacturing capabilities, or human talent. This sharing of resources can lead to cost savings, economies of scale, improved efficiency, and accelerated product development cycles.

Knowledge exchange and innovation: Strategic partnerships often facilitate the exchange of knowledge, expertise, and best practices between organizations. This cross-pollination of ideas and perspectives can fuel innovation, drive product or service improvements, and enhance the competitive advantage of both parties.

Risk mitigation: Partnerships can help organizations spread risk by diversifying their operations, reducing dependency on a single market or customer, or sharing the burden of investment and market entry costs. By teaming up with a complementary partner, companies can mitigate the risks associated with entering unfamiliar territories or pursuing ambitious growth strategies.

Access to new customer segments: Collaborating with organizations that have a different customer base or demographic profile can help companies tap into new customer segments and expand their target market. This is particularly valuable when targeting niche or specialized markets where the partner's expertise or brand recognition can provide a competitive edge.

However, exploring strategic partnerships and collaborations also comes with challenges and risks. It requires careful evaluation of potential partners, alignment of objectives and values, effective communication and coordination, and the establishment of clear governance structures and mechanisms to ensure a fair and equitable relationship.

Expanding into new markets and demographics:

Expanding into new markets and demographics involves the strategic decision and execution of entering previously untapped or underrepresented markets or targeting different customer segments with a company's products or services. This expansion can occur domestically or internationally, depending on the company's growth objectives and market opportunities.

The motivation behind expanding into new markets and demographics is multifaceted and can include the following reasons:

Growth opportunities: By expanding into new markets and demographics, companies can tap into untapped customer segments, increase their customer base, and ultimately drive revenue growth. It allows businesses to capitalize on emerging trends, changing consumer preferences, or unmet needs in different markets.

Diversification: Expanding into new markets and demographics provides a diversification strategy, reducing dependence on a single market or customer base. This helps to spread risks and protect against market-specific fluctuations, economic downturns, or changing regulatory environments. Diversification can also enhance a company's resilience and long-term sustainability.

Competitive advantage: Entering new markets or targeting different demographics can provide a competitive advantage by positioning the company as an early mover, a market disruptor, or a provider of unique offerings. It allows businesses to differentiate themselves from competitors and capture market share before others enter.

Access to new resources: Expanding into new

markets and demographics often grants access to new resources, such as raw materials, talent pools, manufacturing capabilities, distribution networks, or technology hubs. This can lead to operational efficiencies, cost savings, or improved supply chain management.

Globalization and globalization effects: With increasing globalization, companies are exploring international markets to leverage economies of scale, benefit from lower production costs, or gain access to larger customer bases. Expanding into new markets enables businesses to become global players and take advantage of global trade opportunities.

To successfully expand into new markets and demographics, companies need to conduct thorough market research and analysis to understand the cultural, economic, regulatory, and competitive dynamics of the target market. They must adapt their products or services to suit the specific needs and preferences of the new customer segments while considering local regulations and business practices. Furthermore, companies need to develop effective marketing and distribution strategies to reach and engage the target audience.

Expanding into new markets and demographics is a

complex process that requires careful planning, investment, and execution. It may involve establishing local partnerships, building distribution networks, conducting market entry trials, or adapting business models to suit the new market conditions. However, when done successfully, this expansion strategy can fuel business growth, increase market share, and open up new avenues for long-term success.

15

Chapter 15: Monitoring and Managing Your Brand's Reputation

What we will be covering in this chapter:

- Utilizing online reputation management tools
- Responding effectively to negative feedback or crises

Utilizing Online Reputation Management Tools:

In today's digital age, online reputation management has become a crucial aspect of maintaining a positive image for individuals, businesses, and organizations. Online reputation management tools are invaluable resources that can help monitor, track, and improve one's online presence. Here is an elaborate explanation of the benefits and strategies for utilizing these tools effectively:

Monitoring Online Mentions: Online reputation management tools enable individuals or businesses to monitor their online mentions across various platforms, such as social media, review sites, news outlets, and blogs. These tools use advanced algorithms and search capabilities to identify and gather data on brand mentions or discussions related to specific keywords. By staying aware of online conversations, you can proactively address any potential issues or negative feedback.

Tracking Social Media Sentiment: Social media platforms play a significant role in shaping public opinion. Reputation management tools can track sentiment analysis, providing insights into how people perceive your brand or organization. They analyze the tone and context of social media mentions, identifying positive, negative, or neutral sentiment. This information helps you understand public sentiment, identify patterns, and take appropriate actions to manage your reputation effectively.

Online Review Management: Online reviews have a significant impact on a business's reputation. Reputation management tools provide features that help monitor and respond to reviews across various platforms, such as Google My Business, Yelp, TripAdvisor, and industry-specific review sites. These tools allow you to consolidate reviews, receive notifications for new reviews, and respond promptly. Engaging with both positive and negative reviews demonstrates your commitment to customer satisfaction and helps build trust.

Content Management: Reputation management tools assist in managing and optimizing your online content. They provide features to monitor and control search engine results, ensuring that accurate and positive information ranks higher. These tools can identify any negative or misleading content that may harm your reputation and help you take appropriate action to address or remove it.

Competitor Analysis: Online reputation management tools can also provide insights into your competitors' online presence. By monitoring their mentions, reviews, and overall sentiment, you can identify areas where you can differentiate yourself and gain a competitive advantage. Understanding your competitors' reputation management strategies allows you to benchmark your own efforts and make informed decisions to improve your online reputation.

Responding Effectively to Negative Feedback or Crises:

Negative feedback or crises can significantly impact your online reputation, but how you respond to them can make a world of difference. Here are some strategies for effectively addressing negative feedback or managing crises:

Promptness: Timely response is crucial when dealing with negative feedback or crises. Acknowledge the issue as soon as possible to demonstrate that you take customer concerns seriously. Delayed responses can further escalate the situation and damage your reputation. Reputation management tools often provide real-time notifications, ensuring you can address issues promptly.

Empathy and Understanding: Show empathy and understanding towards the concerns raised. Address the customer's complaint or issue with genuine concern, acknowledging their perspective. This demonstrates that you value your customers and are committed to resolving their problems.

Personalization: Tailor your responses to individual situations rather than providing generic replies. Personalized responses show that you are attentive and willing to go the extra mile to address concerns. Use the customer's name and reference specific details to convey your dedication to resolving the issue.

Transparency: Be transparent in your communication. Provide clear explanations of the steps you are taking to address the problem or rectify the situation. Transparency helps build trust and reassures customers that you are committed to resolving their concerns.

Offline Communication: In some cases, it may be more appropriate to take the conversation offline. Provide contact information or a direct point of contact for the customer to discuss their concerns privately. This approach allows for a more personal and in-depth resolution process, demonstrating your commitment to customer satisfaction.

Learning and Improvement: Negative feedback should be seen as an opportunity for growth. Use the feedback to identify areas for improvement within your business or organization. Implement changes based on the feedback received to prevent similar issues from recurring in the future.

By effectively utilizing online reputation management tools and responding to negative feedback or crises with empathy, transparency, and a commitment to resolution, you can mitigate the impact of negative experiences and maintain a positive online reputation.

Example:

XYZ Airlines is a major international airline with a strong online presence. They actively monitor their online reputation using reputation management tools to ensure a positive brand image. One day, a passenger named John had a negative experience during his flight with XYZ Airlines and took to social media to express his dissatisfaction.

Monitoring Online Mentions:
XYZ Airlines utilizes online reputation management tools that continuously monitor social media platforms, review sites, and news outlets for mentions of their brand. They receive real-time notifications whenever there is a new mention related to their airline.

Tracking Social Media Sentiment:
The reputation management tool tracks sentiment analysis and identifies negative mentions or discussions related to XYZ Airlines. Upon detecting

John's negative post, the tool alerts the airline's customer service team about the situation.

Online Review Management:

The reputation management tool consolidates online reviews from various platforms. XYZ Airlines notices that John has also left a negative review on a popular travel review site. Using the tool, they can respond to the review promptly.

Content Management:

The reputation management tool helps XYZ Airlines monitor search engine results related to their brand. They notice that John's social media post and negative review are appearing prominently in search results. The airline takes action to counterbalance this by creating and optimizing positive content, such as blog posts, press releases, and customer testimonials, to improve their online reputation.

Responding to John's Negative Feedback:

Promptness:

Upon receiving the real-time notification about John's post, XYZ Airlines acts promptly. They acknowledge the issue within hours to demonstrate their commitment to resolving customer concerns.

Empathy and Understanding:

In their response, XYZ Airlines empathizes with John's negative experience and expresses understanding of his frustration. They apologize for the inconvenience he faced and assure him that they take his feedback seriously.

Personalization:

The airline addresses John by his name in their response and references specific details from his complaint, showing that they have carefully reviewed his concerns. This personalized approach makes John feel valued as a customer.

Transparency:

XYZ Airlines provides a transparent explanation of the steps they are taking to address the issue. They outline the measures they will implement to prevent similar incidents in the future, such as additional staff training and reviewing their customer service protocols.

Offline Communication:

To provide a more personalized resolution process, XYZ Airlines encourages John to contact their customer service team directly through a private message or a dedicated phone line. This allows for a one-on-one conversation to address his specific concerns and find a suitable solution.

Learning and Improvement:

XYZ Airlines sees John's feedback as an opportunity to improve their services. They take his complaint as constructive criticism and make internal adjustments to their processes to ensure better customer experiences going forward. They also thank him for bringing the issue to their attention and emphasize their commitment to continuous improvement.

By promptly addressing John's negative feedback with empathy, transparency, and personalized communication, XYZ Airlines demonstrates their dedication to customer satisfaction. Utilizing online reputation management tools allows them to stay proactive in managing their online presence, effectively resolving issues, and maintaining a positive brand image.

16

Chapter 16: Innovation and Adaptability in Brand Building

What we will be covering in this chapter:

- Embracing change and staying ahead of market trends
- Evolving your brand to meet evolving customer needs

Embracing Change and Staying Ahead of Market Trends

In today's fast-paced and dynamic business landscape, embracing change and staying ahead of market trends is essential for long-term success and growth. Businesses that resist change or fail to adapt to emerging trends often find themselves falling behind their competitors and struggling to meet the evolving needs of their customers. On the other hand, companies that proactively embrace change and continuously monitor and respond to market trends position themselves as industry leaders, driving innovation and capturing new opportunities.

To effectively embrace change, businesses must foster a culture that values innovation, agility, and a willingness to take risks. This begins with culti-vating a mindset that change is not only inevitable but also presents opportunities for growth. Instead of fearing or resisting change, organizations should view it as a chance to explore new possibilities, improve processes, and create added value for their customers.

Staying ahead of market trends requires a proactive approach to gathering and analyzing relevant data. This involves monitoring industry developments, tracking consumer behavior, and staying informed about emerging technologies and market disruptors. By leveraging data-driven insights, businesses can make informed decisions and anticipate changes before they occur. This allows them to adapt their strategies, products, and services in a timely manner, ensuring they remain relevant and competitive in the market.

One effective way to stay ahead of market trends is to establish strong networks and partnerships within the industry. Engaging in collaborations with other businesses, industry experts, and thought leaders can provide valuable insights and early access to emerging trends. By actively participating in industry events, conferences, and forums, companies can stay connected with the pulse of the market and gain a deeper understanding of customer needs and expectations.

Evolving Your Brand to Meet Evolving Customer Needs

In a rapidly changing business landscape, customer needs and preferences are constantly evolving. To remain successful, brands must adapt and evolve along with their customers. This requires a deep understanding of the target audience and a commitment to continuously assess and meet their changing needs.

The first step in evolving your brand is to conduct thorough market research and gather insights into customer behavior and preferences. This can be done through surveys, focus groups, social listening, and data analysis. By understanding your customers' pain points, desires, and expectations, you can identify gaps in your current offerings and find opportunities to enhance your brand's relevance.

Based on the insights gained from market research, businesses can then develop a customer-centric approach to product development, marketing, and customer service. This involves aligning brand messaging, values, and positioning with the evolving needs and desires of the target audience. By continuously evaluating customer feedback and market trends, brands can identify areas where their products or services may need improvement or modification.

Brand evolution also encompasses adapting to emerging technologies and channels of communication. As new technologies and platforms emerge, customer preferences for interaction and engagement may change. Brands should be proactive in exploring and leveraging these new technologies to create personalized and immersive experiences for their customers. This may involve developing mobile apps, leveraging artificial intelligence, or adopting new communication channels such as social media platforms or chatbots.

Moreover, building and nurturing strong relationships with customers is crucial in evolving your brand. Actively listening to customer feedback, addressing their concerns, and incorporating their suggestions into your brand's offerings demonstrates a commitment to continuous improvement. By fostering a sense of co-creation, brands can establish loyalty and advocacy among their customer base.

In summary, embracing change and staying ahead of market trends is vital for the long-term success of any business. By fostering a culture of innovation, proactively monitoring market trends, and leveraging data-driven insights, companies can position themselves as industry leaders. Evolving your brand to meet evolving customer needs requires a deep understanding of your target audience, a commitment to continuous market research, and a customer-centric approach to product development and marketing. By adapting to changing customer preferences and leveraging emerging technologies, brands can ensure their relevance and success in a dynamic business environment.

Example: Nike's Transformation to a Digital-First Brand

Nike, the multinational sportswear and footwear giant, has successfully embraced change and evolved its brand to meet evolving customer needs by adopting a digital-first strategy. As consumer behavior shifted towards online shopping and digital experiences, Nike recognized the need to adapt its business model and engage with customers through digital platforms.

Embracing Change:

Nike embraced the change by acknowledging the growing influence of technology and e-commerce. The company realized that in order to stay ahead of market trends, it needed to invest in digital technologies and create a seamless online shopping experience for its customers. Nike made significant investments in digital platforms, data analytics, and mobile applications to enhance customer engagement and cater to the evolving needs of its tech-savvy customer base.

Nike+ and Nike App:

To evolve its brand, Nike launched the Nike+ ecosystem, which includes the Nike+ mobile app. This app offers personalized content, training programs, and exclusive products to its users. By leveraging the power of data, Nike gained valuable insights into customer preferences, enabling them to deliver personalized recommendations and tailored experiences.

Connected Footwear:

Nike also introduced connected footwear, such as the Nike Adapt line of self-lacing shoes. These shoes are equipped with sensors and Bluetooth technology, allowing users to customize fit and control their shoes through a smartphone app. This innovative product not only catered to the growing demand for personalized and interactive experiences but also showcased Nike's commitment to embracing technological advancements.

Partnerships and Collaborations:

Nike embraced change by forming strategic partnerships and collaborations with technology companies. For instance, Nike collaborated with Apple to integrate its Nike+ platform with Apple's HealthKit and Apple Watch. This integration allowed users to seamlessly track their fitness activities and connect with the Nike+ community, further enhancing customer engagement and loyalty.

Evolving Customer Needs:

Nike recognized that customers were increasingly seeking personalized and immersive experiences. By leveraging its digital platforms and data-driven insights, Nike evolved its brand to meet these changing needs.

Customization and Co-creation:

Nike introduced customizable products and co-creation experiences to engage customers. Through their Nike By You program, customers can design and personalize their own sneakers by selecting colors, materials, and even adding custom graphics. This initiative taps into the desire for unique and individualized products, fostering a deeper emotional connection with customers.

Community and Social Engagement:

Nike actively engages with its customer community through social media and user-generated content. The company embraces social media platforms as channels for communication, marketing, and gathering customer feedback. By leveraging social media influencers and running targeted campaigns, Nike stays connected with its customer base and fosters a sense of community and belonging.

Data-Driven Decision Making:

Nike uses data analytics to gain insights into customer behavior, preferences, and market trends. By analyzing customer data, Nike can identify emerging trends, anticipate demand, and optimize its product offerings. This data-driven approach enables Nike to make informed decisions, ensuring that its brand evolves in line with customer expectations.

In conclusion, Nike's transformation into a digital-first brand exemplifies the importance of embracing change and evolving to meet evolving customer needs. By investing in digital technologies, offering personalized experiences, and leveraging data-driven insights, Nike has successfully stayed ahead of market trends and positioned itself as an industry leader. The company's focus on innovation, customer engagement, and adapting to emerging technologies has propelled its brand evolution and sustained its competitive advantage in the sportswear industry.

Chapter 17: Measuring Brand Success

W hat we will be covering in this chapter:

- Identifying key performance indicators (KPIs) for brand evaluation
- Analyzing data and making data-driven decisions

Identifying Key Performance Indicators (KPIs) for Brand Evaluation:

Key Performance Indicators (KPIs) are measurable values that indicate how effectively a company is achieving its strategic objectives. When it comes to brand evaluation, KPIs play a crucial role in assessing the success and impact of branding efforts. Here's an elaborate explanation of how to identify

KPIs for brand evaluation:

Define brand objectives: Start by clearly defining your brand objectives. These objectives should align with your overall business goals and reflect what you want your brand to achieve. Examples of brand objectives could include increasing brand awareness, improving brand perception, boosting customer loyalty, or driving brand equity.

Identify relevant metrics: Once you have defined your brand objectives, identify the specific metrics that can effectively measure your progress towards those objectives. These metrics should be quantifiable, trackable, and directly related to your brand's performance. Consider both quantitative metrics (such as sales figures, website traffic, social media engagement) and qualitative metrics (such as customer surveys, brand sentiment analysis, brand reputation).

Align with brand strategy: Ensure that the chosen KPIs align with your brand strategy. Your brand strategy outlines the key elements that differentiate your brand and create a unique value proposition. The KPIs you select should reflect and measure the success of these strategic elements. For example, if your brand strategy focuses on innovation, a relevant KPI could be the number of new products or services introduced.

Prioritize KPIs: Determine the most critical KPIs that have the highest impact on your brand's performance. Not all metrics are equally important, so prioritize the ones that directly contribute to your brand's success. Consider the level of influence each KPI has on your brand objectives and select a manageable number of key metrics to focus on.

Establish benchmarks and targets: Set benchmarks and targets for each KPI to track your brand's progress over time. These benchmarks can be industry standards, historical data, or competitor performance. Establishing targets allows you to measure the effectiveness of your brand initiatives and provides a clear direction for improvement.

Continuous evaluation and refinement: Regularly review and evaluate your chosen KPIs to ensure they remain relevant and aligned with your brand objectives. As your brand evolves and market dynamics change, some metrics may lose relevance, and new ones may emerge. Be open to refining your KPIs to ensure they accurately reflect your brand's performance and guide your decision-making process.

Analyzing Data and Making Data-Driven Decisions:

In today's data-driven business landscape, organizations have access to vast amounts of data that can provide valuable insights and inform decision-making processes. Here's an elaborate explanation of how to analyze data and make data-driven decisions:

Collect relevant data: Start by collecting relevant data that is aligned with the specific problem or decision you are trying to address. This data can come from various sources, such as customer surveys, sales reports, website analytics, social media metrics, market research, or internal databases. Ensure the data is accurate, reliable, and comprehensive.

Define objectives and questions: Clearly define the objectives and questions you want to answer through data analysis. This ensures focus and clarity in the analysis process. Identify the specific insights you need to make informed decisions. For example, if you are analyzing customer satisfaction, you might want to understand factors influencing customer loyalty or identify areas for improvement.

Clean and organize the data: Data cleaning is a

crucial step to ensure the accuracy and quality of your analysis. Remove any duplicates, inconsistencies, or irrelevant data points. Organize the data in a structured manner, ensuring it is ready for analysis. This may involve data transformation, normalization, or aggregation.

Choose appropriate analysis methods: Select the appropriate analysis methods based on your objectives and the nature of the data. This can include descriptive analysis (summarizing data using statistics and visualizations), diagnostic analysis (identifying patterns and relationships), predictive analysis (forecasting future trends), or prescriptive analysis (providing recommendations based on data insights). Utilize statistical techniques, data visualization tools, and machine learning algorithms if necessary.

Interpret and derive insights: Analyze the data to uncover meaningful insights and patterns. Look for trends, correlations, anomalies, or any significant findings that can provide valuable information. Ensure that you interpret the data objectively, considering multiple perspectives and potential biases. Use data visualization techniques to present the findings effectively and facilitate understanding.

Make data-driven decisions: Once you have derived insights from the data analysis, use them to inform your decision-making process. Combine the data insights with your domain knowledge and expertise to make informed, data-driven decisions. Consider the implications, risks, and potential outcomes of each decision. Communicate the findings and recommendations to relevant stakeholders, ensuring transparency and clarity.

Monitor and iterate: After implementing your decisions, continuously monitor the results and outcomes. Measure the impact of your decisions against the desired objectives and evaluate whether the expected outcomes are being achieved. If necessary, iterate and refine your approach based on the ongoing analysis and feedback.

Remember that data analysis and data-driven decision-making are iterative processes. Embrace a culture of learning and improvement, where data is consistently collected, analyzed, and used to optimize your business strategies and operations.

Let's consider a real-life example of a company in the retail industry that wants to evaluate its brand performance and make data-driven decisions.

Define brand objectives: The company's brand objectives include increasing brand awareness, improving customer loyalty, and driving online sales.

Identify relevant metrics: The company selects metrics such as brand recognition surveys, customer satisfaction scores, repeat purchase rate, website traffic, conversion rate, and social media engagement as key indicators of its brand performance.

Align with brand strategy: The company's brand strategy revolves around providing personalized shopping experiences and excellent customer service. As a result, it focuses on metrics like customer satisfaction scores and repeat purchase rate to measure the success of these strategic elements.

Prioritize KPIs: The company prioritizes the customer satisfaction score and repeat purchase rate as the primary KPIs since they directly contribute to improving brand loyalty and driving sales.

Establish benchmarks and targets: The company sets a benchmark for customer satisfaction score based on industry standards and competitors' performance. It also sets a target for increasing the repeat purchase rate by 10% within the next quarter.

Continuous evaluation and refinement: The company regularly reviews the selected KPIs, considering market changes and customer feedback. It refines the KPIs by adding new metrics such as Net Promoter Score (NPS) based on the evolving needs of the business and its brand strategy.

Now, let's move on to analyzing data and making data-driven decisions:

Collect relevant data: The company collects data from customer surveys, point-of-sale systems, website analytics, and social media platforms. It gathers information on customer satisfaction scores, purchase history, website traffic, conversion rates, and social media engagement.

Define objectives and questions: The company aims to understand the factors influencing customer satisfaction, identify areas for improvement in customer service, and optimize its online sales funnel. It formulates questions like "What are the main drivers of customer satisfaction?" and "How can we improve the conversion rate on our website?"

Clean and organize the data: The company cleans the data by removing duplicate entries, handling missing values, and ensuring consistency across different data sources. It organizes the data in a structured format for analysis.

Choose appropriate analysis methods: The company utilizes statistical analysis techniques, such as regression analysis and correlation analysis, to identify the factors influencing customer satisfaction. It also uses data visualization tools to create visual representations of website traffic patterns and conversion funnels.

Interpret and derive insights: Through data analysis, the company discovers that personalized customer service and quick response times significantly impact customer satisfaction. It also finds that the checkout process on the website has a high abandonment rate, affecting the conversion rate.

Make data-driven decisions: Based on the insights gained, the company decides to invest in training its customer service representatives to deliver personalized experiences and reduce response times. It also focuses on optimizing the checkout process on the website by simplifying steps and offering more payment options.

Monitor and iterate: The company monitors the impact of its decisions by tracking changes in customer satisfaction scores, repeat purchase rate, website traffic, and conversion rate. It continues to collect and analyze data, making further adjustments to its strategies as needed.

By using KPIs for brand evaluation and analyzing data to make data-driven decisions, the company can enhance its brand performance, improve customer satisfaction, and drive online sales effectively.

Let's consider another real-life example, this time focusing on a software-as-a-service (SaaS) company that wants to evaluate its brand performance and make data-driven decisions.

Define brand objectives: The SaaS company's brand objectives include increasing brand recognition, expanding its customer base, and improving customer satisfaction and retention.

Identify relevant metrics: The company selects metrics such as brand awareness surveys, customer acquisition rate, customer churn rate, customer satisfaction score (CSAT), and Net Promoter Score (NPS) as key indicators of its brand performance.

Align with brand strategy: The company's brand strategy revolves around delivering a user-friendly and reliable software product, as well as providing exceptional customer support. Therefore, it focuses on metrics such as CSAT and NPS to measure customer satisfaction and loyalty.

Prioritize KPIs: The company prioritizes customer satisfaction score (CSAT) and Net Promoter Score (NPS) as the primary KPIs, as they directly reflect customer sentiment and loyalty towards the brand.

Establish benchmarks and targets: The company sets a benchmark for CSAT based on industry standards and competitor performance. It also sets a target to achieve a Net Promoter Score of 40 within the next year.

Continuous evaluation and refinement: The company regularly reviews and refines its selected KPIs based on customer feedback, market changes, and business goals. It may consider adding additional metrics such as customer lifetime value (CLV) or customer referral rates to gain deeper insights into brand performance.

Moving on to analyzing data and making data-driven decisions:

Collect relevant data: The company collects data

from customer surveys, support ticket systems, user analytics, and customer feedback channels. It gathers information on CSAT scores, NPS ratings, customer acquisition rates, churn rates, and usage patterns.

Define objectives and questions: The company aims to understand the factors influencing customer satisfaction, identify pain points in the customer journey, and optimize its customer acquisition and retention strategies. It formulates questions like "What are the main drivers of customer satisfaction?" and "How can we improve customer onboarding to reduce churn?"

Clean and organize the data: The company cleans the data by removing duplicates, handling missing values, and ensuring data consistency. It organizes the data in a structured format for analysis.

Choose appropriate analysis methods: The company employs statistical techniques such as regression analysis and correlation analysis to identify the factors impacting customer satisfaction and churn rates. It also uses cohort analysis to understand user behavior over time.

Interpret and derive insights: Through data analysis,

the company discovers that quick response times and effective issue resolution have a significant impact on customer satisfaction. It also finds that customers who onboard successfully within the first week have a higher likelihood of long-term retention.

Make data-driven decisions: Based on the insights gained, the company decides to invest in improving its support response times and implementing proactive customer onboarding strategies. It may also consider enhancing its knowledge base or providing additional training resources to address common customer pain points.

Monitor and iterate: The company continuously monitors the impact of its decisions by tracking changes in CSAT scores, NPS ratings, customer acquisition rates, and churn rates. It iterates on its strategies based on ongoing analysis, customer feedback, and market dynamics.

By using relevant KPIs for brand evaluation and analyzing data to make data-driven decisions, the SaaS company can improve its brand performance, enhance customer satisfaction, and drive customer acquisition and retention more effectively.

18

Chapter 18: Branding Beyond Products and Services

W hat we will be covering in this chapter:

- Extending your brand to include corporate social responsibility
- Making a positive impact on society through your brand

Extending your brand to include corporate social responsibility (CSR) means incorporating social and environmental initiatives into your business practices and brand identity. It involves leveraging your brand's influence and resources to make a positive impact on society. Here are some examples of how brands can extend themselves through CSR:

Environmental Sustainability: Many brands are

adopting sustainable practices to reduce their carbon footprint and preserve natural resources. For example, a clothing brand might use eco-friendly materials, implement recycling programs, or reduce water consumption during manufacturing.

Philanthropy and Charitable Partnerships: Brands can engage in philanthropic activities by supporting nonprofit organizations or partnering with charitable initiatives. They can donate a percentage of their profits to causes that align with their brand values. For instance, a food company might collaborate with a local food bank to provide meals for those in need.

Employee Volunteer Programs: Brands can encourage their employees to participate in volunteer activities during work hours or provide paid volunteer time off. This allows employees to contribute to their communities and aligns the brand with positive social change.

Cause-Related Marketing: Brands can associate their products or services with a social cause to raise awareness and support. For example, a beverage company might donate a portion of each purchase to a cancer research organization or use packaging that promotes environmental awareness.

Ethical Supply Chain: Brands can prioritize ethical sourcing and fair trade practices by working with suppliers and partners who adhere to responsible labor and production standards. This ensures that their products are made under ethical conditions and supports the welfare of workers.

Education and Awareness Campaigns: Brands can use their influence to educate the public on important social issues or promote awareness campaigns. For instance, a technology company might launch a campaign to raise awareness about online safety or digital literacy.

Diversity and Inclusion: Brands can foster diversity and inclusion within their organization and promote these values externally. This can be achieved by ensuring a diverse workforce, representing various communities in marketing materials, or supporting initiatives that promote equal opportunities.

By incorporating CSR initiatives into their brand strategy, businesses can not only make a positive impact on society but also strengthen their brand reputation, build customer loyalty, and attract socially conscious consumers. It's important for brands to authentically align their CSR efforts with their core values and consistently communicate their commitment to social responsibility.

Here's a real-life example of a brand that has successfully extended its identity to include corporate social responsibility:

Patagonia: Patagonia is an outdoor clothing and gear company known for its commitment to environmental and social responsibility. The brand has implemented several initiatives that align with its values:

Environmental Sustainability: Patagonia has been a leader in promoting environmental sustainability. They have taken steps to reduce their ecological footprint by using recycled materials in their products, implementing responsible manufacturing processes, and supporting initiatives to protect public lands and promote conservation.

Common Threads Initiative: Patagonia launched the Common Threads Initiative, encouraging customers to reduce consumption by repairing and reusing their clothing. They offer free repairs for their products and promote extending the life of their garments through proper care and maintenance.

Worn Wear Program: Patagonia operates the Worn Wear program, which encourages customers to buy and sell used Patagonia gear. They provide resources and tutorials on repairing and maintaining products, promoting a culture of reuse and reducing waste.

1% for the Planet: Since 1985, Patagonia has committed to donating at least 1% of its sales to environmental causes through the 1% for the Planet initiative. This has resulted in millions of dollars being donated to various environmental organizations and projects worldwide.

Political Activism: Patagonia has used its brand platform to advocate for environmental causes and engage in political activism. They have run campaigns urging customers to take action on issues such as climate change and public lands protection.

These examples demonstrate how Patagonia has extended its brand to include corporate social responsibility. By aligning their business practices and initiatives with their core values, Patagonia has created a strong brand identity that resonates with environmentally conscious consumers and sets them apart in the outdoor apparel industry.

Chapter 19: Cultivating a Brand Culture

What we will be covering in this chapter:

- Building a strong internal brand culture among employees
- Aligning your team's values with your brand's values

Building a strong internal brand culture among employees is crucial for creating a cohesive and united workforce that is aligned with the organization's values and goals. When employees identify with and embrace the brand culture, it can lead to increased engagement, productivity, and overall job satisfaction. Here are some ways to build a strong internal brand culture, along with examples:

Clearly define and communicate your brand values: Clearly articulate the core values and principles that define your brand. These values should reflect the organization's mission, vision, and purpose. Communicate these values to your employees through various channels, such as company meetings, training sessions, internal newsletters, and digital platforms. For example, if your brand values include innovation and creativity, you can organize brainstorming sessions or innovation challenges to encourage employees to think outside the box.

Lead by example: Leaders and managers play a crucial role in shaping the internal brand culture. They should embody the brand values and behaviors themselves and demonstrate them in their everyday interactions with employees. This creates a culture of consistency and sets the tone for others to follow. For instance, if one of your brand values is transparency, leaders should openly share information, encourage open communication, and be accessible to employees.

Involve employees in shaping the brand culture: Empower employees to actively participate in shaping the internal brand culture. Seek their input and ideas on how to embody the brand values in their day-to-day work and foster a sense of ownership. For example, you can create employee-led committees or focus groups that are responsible for organizing cultural events or initiatives that align with the brand values.

Provide training and development opportunities: Invest in training and development programs that reinforce the brand values and behaviors. This can include workshops, seminars, or online courses that educate employees on the brand's history, values, and desired behaviors. For instance, if one of your brand values is exceptional customer service, provide customer service training to equip employees with the necessary skills and knowledge to deliver on that promise.

Recognize and reward behaviors aligned with brand values: Establish recognition and reward systems that acknowledge employees who exemplify the brand values in their work. This can be done through employee recognition programs, performance evaluations, or incentive programs. For example, you can create an "Employee of the Month" award that celebrates individuals who consistently demonstrate the brand values in their interactions with colleagues and customers.

Foster a positive and inclusive work environment:

Create a work environment that fosters positivity, collaboration, and inclusivity. Encourage teamwork, celebrate diversity, and provide opportunities for employees to connect and build relationships. This can be achieved through team-building activities, employee resource groups, or social events. For example, you can organize team-building exercises that promote collaboration and reinforce the importance of working together towards a common goal.

Communicate and reinforce the brand culture consistently: Consistent communication is essential to reinforce the brand culture among employees. Use various communication channels, such as internal newsletters, intranet portals, or digital signage, to regularly share stories, updates, and success stories that highlight how employees are living the brand values. For instance, you can feature employee spotlights or testimonials that showcase individuals who embody the brand culture.

Remember that building a strong internal brand culture is an ongoing process. It requires consistent effort, engagement, and reinforcement to ensure that employees internalize and live the brand values.

Here are two real-life examples of companies

that have successfully built a strong internal brand culture among their employees:

Zappos:

Zappos, an online shoe and clothing retailer, is well-known for its exceptional customer service and vibrant company culture. Zappos has a strong internal brand culture centered around core values like delivering WOW through service, embracing and driving change, and creating fun and a little weirdness. They have successfully aligned their team's values with their brand's values in the following ways:

Employee empowerment: Zappos empowers its employees to go above and beyond in delivering exceptional customer service. Customer service representatives have the authority to make decisions without seeking managerial approval, which encourages them to embody the brand's values and create memorable experiences for customers.

Cultural events and activities: Zappos organizes various cultural events and activities to foster a positive and inclusive work environment. They have a dedicated Culture Team responsible for organizing events like "Culture Blast" and "Zapponian

Olympics" that promote teamwork, camaraderie, and fun. These events help employees connect with each other and reinforce the brand's value of creating fun and a little weirdness.

Google:

Google is renowned for its strong internal brand culture, characterized by innovation, creativity, and a focus on employee well-being. Google has aligned its team's values with the brand's values in the following ways:

Innovation-driven work environment: Google encourages employees to think creatively and pursue innovative ideas. They provide employees with dedicated time, known as "20% time," to work on personal projects that align with the company's goals. This initiative fosters a culture of innovation and empowers employees to contribute their ideas and make an impact.

Employee perks and well-being programs: Google places a strong emphasis on employee well-being and provides various perks and programs to support their physical and mental health. These include on-site fitness centers, free healthy meals, mindfulness programs, and flexible work arrangements. By prioritizing employee well-being, Google demonstrates its commitment to the brand value of caring for its people.

These examples illustrate how Zappos and Google have successfully built strong internal brand cultures by aligning their team's values with their brand's values. Through empowerment, cultural events, innovation-driven environments, and employee well-being initiatives, these companies have created cohesive and engaged workforces that embody their brand values.

20

Chapter 20: Sustaining and Evolving Your Brand

What we will be covering in this chapter:

- Strategies for long-term brand sustainability
- Embracing innovation and continuously improving your brand

Strategies for long-term brand sustainability:

Define your brand purpose: To ensure long-term brand sustainability, it's crucial to have a clear and compelling purpose. Define why your brand exists beyond just selling products or services. Determine the values, beliefs, and principles that guide your brand and resonate with your target audience. A strong brand purpose creates an emotional connection with consumers and fosters loyalty.

Build a strong brand identity: Develop a consistent and distinctive brand identity that represents your purpose and resonates with your target market. This includes creating a memorable brand name, designing a visually appealing logo, choosing appropriate colors and typography, and developing a unique brand voice. Consistency across all brand touchpoints helps establish brand recognition and builds trust among consumers.

Understand your target audience: Conduct thorough market research to gain a deep understanding of your target audience's needs, preferences, and behaviors. Identify their pain points, aspirations, and motivations. By understanding your customers, you can tailor your brand messaging, product offerings, and customer experiences to meet their expectations, thereby enhancing brand loyalty and long-term sustainability.

Deliver exceptional customer experiences: Consistently provide superior customer experiences at every touchpoint. Invest in customer service training, adopt efficient communication channels, and personalize interactions to create a positive and memorable experience. Address customer feedback promptly and strive to exceed expectations. Positive experiences lead to customer loyalty, positive word-of-mouth, and repeat business, all of which contribute to long-term brand sustainability.

Build brand authenticity and transparency: In today's era of heightened consumer consciousness, authenticity and transparency are paramount. Be genuine and true to your brand purpose, values, and promises. Avoid misleading or exaggerated claims and communicate openly about your business practices, sourcing, and social or environmental initiatives. Transparency builds trust and fosters long-term relationships with consumers.

Foster brand advocacy: Encourage your satisfied customers to become brand advocates. Provide opportunities for them to share their positive experiences through testimonials, reviews, and user-generated content. Leverage social media platforms and influencer partnerships to amplify your brand message. Brand advocates can significantly impact brand sustainability by spreading positive word-of-mouth and attracting new customers.

Monitor and adapt to market trends: Stay abreast of market trends, technological advancements, and evolving consumer preferences. Regularly assess your brand's positioning in the market and compare it with competitors. Continuously innovate and adapt your products, services, and marketing strategies to remain relevant and meet changing consumer demands. Embrace new technologies and platforms that can enhance your brand's visibility and engagement with your target audience.

Embracing innovation and continuously improving your brand:

Encourage a culture of innovation: Foster a work environment that encourages creativity, curiosity, and continuous improvement. Empower employees to share their ideas and provide a platform for collaboration. Reward and recognize innovative thinking and risk-taking. By embracing a culture of innovation, you can tap into the collective intelligence of your team and drive meaningful changes that contribute to the growth and sustainability of your brand.

Embrace emerging technologies: Stay updated on emerging technologies relevant to your industry and explore how they can enhance your brand's offerings and customer experience. For example, artificial intelligence (AI), machine learning, and data analytics can provide valuable insights into consumer behavior and enable personalized marketing strategies. Adopting new technologies can streamline operations, improve efficiency, and drive innovation across various brand touchpoints.

Conduct market research and consumer insights: Regularly conduct market research and gather consumer insights to understand emerging trends, changing customer preferences, and unmet needs. Use this information to identify gaps in the market and develop innovative solutions that address those gaps. Feedback from customers, surveys, focus groups, and social listening tools can provide valuable insights for continuous brand improvement.

Invest in product development and R&D: Allocate resources to research and development (R&D) to continuously improve existing products and develop new ones. Monitor customer feedback, identify areas for improvement, and incorporate customer insights into product development cycles. Conduct thorough testing and quality control to ensure your products meet or exceed customer expectations. Continuous product innovation helps your brand stay competitive and relevant in the market.

Collaborate with industry experts and partners: Foster partnerships and collaborations with industry experts, startups, and other brands to leverage their expertise and innovative solutions. Joint ventures, co-creation initiatives, and strategic alliances can lead to new product offerings, expanded market reach, and enhanced brand reputation. Collaborations also allow you to tap into different perspectives and accelerate innovation within your brand.

Monitor and analyze brand performance: Establish key performance indicators (KPIs) to measure the success and impact of your brand initiatives. Regularly monitor and analyze brand performance metrics, such as sales growth, customer satisfaction, brand awareness, and market share. Use these insights to identify areas for improvement and to refine your strategies. Data-driven decision-making enables you to adapt quickly to market changes and continuously improve your brand.

By implementing these strategies for long-term brand sustainability and embracing innovation, your brand can remain relevant, resilient, and successful in an ever-changing business landscape. Remember, sustaining a brand is an ongoing process that requires adaptability, customer focus, and a commitment to continuous improvement.

21

The Final Chapter: Example and a working plan + framework

B uilding a brand from inception to the final output involves a series of steps and considerations. Let's explore each stage with real-life examples to illustrate the process.

Brand Inception and Research:
At the inception stage, it is essential to define the brand's purpose, target audience, and market positioning. Conduct thorough market research to identify market gaps, consumer needs, and competitor landscape.

Example: Tesla, the electric vehicle (EV) company, was founded with a clear brand purpose: to accelerate the world's transition to sustainable energy. Through extensive research, Tesla recognized the growing demand for electric vehicles and identified an opportunity to disrupt the automotive industry with innovative EV technology.

Brand Identity Development:
Create a strong brand identity that embodies the brand's values, personality, and visual elements. This includes designing a logo, choosing colors and typography, and establishing brand guidelines.

Example: Apple is renowned for its sleek and minimalist brand identity. The bitten apple logo and its clean, sophisticated product design reflect the brand's focus on simplicity, innovation, and user-friendly experiences.

Brand Messaging and Positioning:
Craft compelling brand messaging that communicates the brand's unique value proposition and resonates with the target audience. Develop a brand positioning statement that differentiates the brand from competitors.

Example: Nike's brand messaging revolves around inspiring athletes with its "Just Do It" slogan. By associating the brand with a mindset of determination and overcoming obstacles, Nike has positioned itself as a symbol of athletic excellence and motivation.

Product Development and Launch:

Develop products or services that align with the brand's purpose and target audience's needs. Ensure consistent quality and innovation throughout the product development process. Plan a strategic launch to create anticipation and generate buzz.

Example: Airbnb disrupted the hospitality industry by offering a platform for people to rent out their homes or spare rooms. By leveraging the sharing economy and focusing on unique experiences, Airbnb introduced a new way of traveling and positioned itself as an alternative to traditional accommodations.

Customer Experience and Engagement:

Deliver exceptional customer experiences at every touchpoint. Develop customer-centric policies, invest in customer service training, and create seamless interactions across online and offline channels.

Example: Zappos, an online shoe and clothing retailer, built its brand by prioritizing customer service. Their commitment to going above and beyond customer expectations, including free shipping and a 365-day return policy, has earned them a reputation for exceptional customer experiences.

Marketing and Brand Promotion:
   Implement a comprehensive marketing strategy to raise brand awareness, attract customers, and build brand equity. Utilize various channels such as digital marketing, social media, influencer partnerships, and traditional advertising.

Example: Coca-Cola has successfully built a global brand through consistent and memorable marketing campaigns. From the iconic "Share a Coke" personalized bottles to heartwarming holiday ads, Coca-Cola's marketing efforts evoke emotions and reinforce its brand values of happiness and togetherness.

Brand Evolution and Adaptation:
   Continuously monitor market trends, consumer feedback, and emerging technologies to adapt the brand strategy and offerings. Innovate and introduce new products or services to stay relevant and meet evolving customer needs.

Example: Amazon began as an online bookstore but evolved into a technology and e-commerce giant, continuously expanding its product range and services. By embracing emerging technologies, such as voice assistants (Alexa) and cloud computing (AWS), Amazon has diversified its business while maintaining its customer-centric focus.

Throughout this journey, it is crucial to maintain brand consistency, authenticity, and a commitment to delivering value to customers. Building a brand is an ongoing process that requires continuous adaptation, innovation, and nurturing of customer relationships to ensure long-term success.

Working Plan:

Here's a working plan outlining the steps to build a brand from step 1 to the final output:

- **Brand Inception and Research:**
- Define the brand's purpose, values, and target audience.
- Conduct market research to identify consumer needs, market gaps, and competitor analysis.
- Set clear goals and objectives for the brand-building process.

- **Brand Identity Development:**
- Develop a strong brand name, logo, and visual

identity that align with the brand's purpose and target audience.

- Choose appropriate colors, typography, and design elements that reflect the brand's personality.
- Create brand guidelines to maintain consistency across all brand touchpoints.

- **Brand Messaging and Positioning:**
- Craft a compelling brand story that communicates the brand's unique value proposition.
- Develop key messages that resonate with the target audience.
- Determine the brand's positioning in the market, highlighting its differentiating factors.

- **Product Development and Launch:**
- Develop products or services that align with the brand's purpose and target audience's needs.
- Ensure consistent quality, innovation, and unique features throughout the product development process.
- Plan a strategic product launch, including promotional activities, media outreach, and part-

nerships to generate excitement and awareness.

- **Customer Experience and Engagement:**
- Implement customer-centric policies and processes to deliver exceptional experiences.
- Train customer service teams to provide personalized and efficient support.
- Create a seamless and consistent customer journey across all touchpoints, including online and offline interactions.

- **Marketing and Brand Promotion:**
- Develop a comprehensive marketing strategy aligned with the brand's target audience and objectives.
- Utilize various marketing channels such as digital marketing, social media, content marketing, and traditional advertising.
- Leverage influencer partnerships, brand ambassadors, and strategic collaborations to amplify brand reach and credibility.

- **Brand Evolution and Adaptation:**
- Continuously monitor market trends, consumer feedback, and emerging technologies.
- Adapt the brand strategy and offerings to meet evolving customer needs.
- Innovate and introduce new products or services while maintaining brand consistency and value.

- **Monitoring and Evaluation:**
- Establish key performance indicators (KPIs) to track the success of brand-building efforts.
- Regularly monitor and analyze brand performance metrics, consumer feedback, and market trends.
- Use insights to refine brand strategies, improve customer experiences, and drive continuous improvement.

To turn the brand-building plan into a reality, you can follow a framework that ensures effective implementation and execution. Here's a framework to guide you through the process:

Establish Leadership and Team:

Assign a dedicated team or individual responsible for overseeing the brand-building process.

Ensure clear roles and responsibilities are defined for each team member.

Provide leadership and support to the team, fostering a collaborative and motivated work environment.

Set Objectives and Key Results (OKRs):

Clearly define measurable objectives and key results for each stage of the brand-building process.

Align OKRs with the overall business goals and ensure they are specific, measurable, attainable, relevant, and time-bound (SMART).

Resource Allocation:

Identify the necessary resources, budget, and tools required to execute the brand-building plan.

Allocate resources effectively to different stages and activities, ensuring optimal utilization.

Consider both financial and human resources required for successful implementation.

Implementation Plan:

Break down the brand-building plan into actionable

tasks and create a timeline for each stage.

Assign responsibilities and deadlines for each task, ensuring clear accountability.

Regularly review and update the implementation plan based on progress and evolving requirements.

Collaboration and Communication:

Foster open and effective communication channels within the team and stakeholders involved in the brand-building process.

Encourage collaboration and knowledge sharing to leverage diverse perspectives and expertise.

Conduct regular meetings, progress updates, and feedback sessions to ensure everyone is aligned and informed.

Execution and Quality Control:

Implement each stage of the brand-building plan according to the defined timeline and tasks.

Ensure consistent quality and adherence to brand guidelines throughout the execution process.

Conduct regular quality control checks to maintain brand standards and make necessary adjustments as needed.

Measurement and Evaluation:

Continuously monitor and measure the progress of the brand-building activities against the defined objectives and KPIs.

Collect relevant data and feedback to evaluate the effectiveness of each stage and make data-driven decisions.

Regularly review and analyze the results to identify areas of improvement and adjust strategies accordingly.

Iteration and Continuous Improvement:

Embrace a culture of continuous improvement and adaptability throughout the brand-building process.

Learn from successes and failures, and apply insights gained to refine strategies and tactics.

Incorporate customer feedback and market trends into ongoing iterations to ensure the brand remains relevant and resonates with the target audience.

By following this framework, you can effectively execute the brand-building plan, monitor progress, and make informed adjustments to ensure successful implementation and long-term brand sustainability. Remember to adapt the framework based on the specific needs and characteristics of your brand

and industry.